S · P · U · N · K

SPUNK

THE SELECTED STORIES OF
ZORA NEALE HURSTON

TURTLE ISLAND FOUNDATION BERKELEY CALIFORNIA

ISBN : 0-913666-79-3 Trade Paperback

"Spunk" was first published in *Opportunity Magazine*, June, 1925, and was reprinted later that same year in *The New Negro*, edited by Alain Locke (Albert and Charles Boni: New York, 1925). "Isis" was first published in *Opportunity Magazine*, December, 1924, under the original title, "Drenched in Light." "Muttsy" was first published in *Fire!!*, #1 (November, 1926), and has been republished since in a number of anthologies. "The Gilded Six-Bits" first appeared in *Story*, #3, (August, 1933), and has been republished since in a number of anthologies. "Cock Robin Beale Street" was first published in *Southern Literary Message*, #3, (July, 1942). "Story in Harlem Slang" was first published in *American Mercury*, #45, (July, 1942) and has been republished since in a number of anthologies. "Book of Harlem" is published in this collection for the first time.

SPUNK is published by Turtle Island Foundation for the Netzahualcoyotl Historical Society, a non-profit educational corporation engaged in the multi-cultural study of New World history and literature. For more information, please address: Turtle Island Foundation, 2845 Buena Vista Way, Berkeley, CA 94708

Cover design by Dennis Gallagher
Book design by Eileen Callahan O Malley
    and David Orion Callahan

Also available by Zora Neale Hurston from Turtle Island:
TELL MY HORSE and THE SANCTIFIED CHURCH.

• •

C · O · N · T · E · N · T · S

FOREWORD

In June, 1955, Zora Neale Hurston, American writer extraordinaire, began still another bold and original writing project. "I know you will be startled at my choice of subject," she then wrote a friend, "but I came here to Eau Gallie (Florida), a quiet little spot, to do a work I have had in contemplation for some years now, a life of Herod the Great."

The author knew that, once again, she was about to ruffle more than a few sacred feathers. "Being bred and born to Sunday school, as I was, I know you will immediately think of Herod as the fiend who slaughtered the babies around Bethlehem in an attempt to do away with the infant Jesus."

But was this the real, *historical* Herod, Hurston asked? No, indeed. The real, historical Herod had been the subject of vicious and unfair reporting. "I first became interested in the real Herod while casually looking up another matter. I then came across the following statement — 'Scholars now agree that there is no historical basis for the legend of the slaughter of the innocents by Herod.' "

"I soon learned," Hurston continued, "that this man, whom I had always thought of as a mean little butcher, was, in fact, a highly-cultivated, thoroughly Hellenized citizen of his time, the handsomest man of his era, the greatest soldier of Southwest Asia, the ablest administrator, generous both of spirit and materially, Herod the Over-Bold, Herod of the Sunlike-Splendor."

But why, then, the vicious reporting?

"As I read on," Hurston reported, "I began to perceive why the priestly scribes detested this child of Kings. You must recall just how bound the priesthood was by tradition during that era. On returning from the Babylonian captivity, the priesthood had attempted to shut Judea in. Hellenism was then perceived as a terrible threat. The stranger was considered an absolute taboo."

Hurston had located her answer. "Herod's father had been a close friend to Julius Caesar, Pompey, Marc Antony. Place this over against a priesthood bent on maintaining their ancient rule over the nation, and you can see the conflict. Herod had introduced the arts of Greece — sculpture, painting, drama, architecture, universal education, and even athletics, building local amphitheatres to host the Olympic games. And the nation took to these things like ducks to water.

"The people loved Herod for this, and threw garlands of flowers at him whenever he appeared in the streets.

"You can see now more clearly the real feelings of the traditionalist minority. Herod was perceived as a threat to their very way of life. And yet it is the traditionalists, the priestly scribes, who have provided us with most of the historic records which survive from that time.

"Herod was a transitional figure," Hurston concluded, "perhaps *the* transitional figure between Judaism and Christianity in that particular part of the world." Somewhat of a transitional figure herself, Hurston was thrilled to tell the real story of Herod.

*

Zora Neale Hurston's *Life of Herod the Great* is a work of some four hundred pages, over three hundred pages of which have been so badly transfigured by fire damage as to make the manuscript as a whole ultimately indecipherable. One fascinating section has however survived. In this section Hurston dramatizes the final encounter between Herod, the Hellenic visionary, and the trumped-up charges levelled against him by Hyrcanus, and the other tradition-bound priests. Although Hurston had finished with the short story form by the time she came to write *Herod*, this encounter seems important enough — in some ways almost autobiographical enough — to be included as an appendix to this present volume.

Hurston's *Herod* book became the central driving project force during the last creative period of her life. During this period the incomparable Zora Neale completed a short, as of yet unpublished, important essay on Florida's mostly black migrant farm workers; wrote, and saw performed, a special gospel and folk musical recital; composed another play; discussed with represetatives of the late Walter O'Malley the possibility of writing an essay on the first colored baseball players O'Malley was just then introducing into his Brooklyn Dodger farm system; wrote, even, Winston Churchill to request that he provide an introduction to the Herod Book (an invitation Churchill warmly yet respectfully declined); and generally grew so self-reliant in her politics, so singularly determined in her belief in the dignity and independence of Afro-American culture, that she came to vigorously and publicly oppose the famous Supreme Court desegregation ruling, *Brown vs. Topeka Board of Education.*

"I had promised God, and some other responsible characters, including a bunch of bishops," Hurston wrote the *Orlando Sentinel*, "that I was not going to part my lips concerning the United States Supreme Court decision on ending segregation in the public schools of the South . . . I break my silence just this once . . . The whole matter revolves around the self-respect of my people. How much satisfaction can I get from a court order for somebody to associate with me who does not wish me near them? ... I regard the ruling of the United States Supreme Court as insulting rather than honoring my race."

Although critics never could follow all of her somewhat surprising turnings, Hurston remained bodacious right to the very end.

*

The stories contained in *Spunk* include almost all of Hurston's early Eatonville writings, the work which first brought Zora Neale to the attention of a national audience. From the early "Muttsy" and "Isis," to the later "Spunk," and "The Gilded Six-Bits," the reader can literally witness Zora Neale Hurston grow into the assured, and enormously insightful writer which she became at the very height of her powers. With these early stories, Zora first lit up the sky, becoming one of the very brightest stars in the Harlem Renaissance which flashed across America during the later days of the 1920's.

For the next thirty years, Hurston's primary writing energy was directed into her novels and into her Southern folklore books. With a writer like Hurston, however, the line between folklore and fiction simply does not exist; literature is continually returning to its aboriginal and folk culture roots; a confidence man is always becoming a trickster is always becoming a confidence man; and certain later parables and experiments, such as "Cock Robin Beale Street," "Story in Harlem Slang," and "Book of Harlem," perfectly exhibit the ways in which, in Hurston's imagination, real life is constantly turning into folklore, and folklore is turning back into real life all the time. It is an amazing gift, very near to the core of the particular genius which this remarkable author ultimately came to possess.

From Eatonville, then, the westbound train to New Orleans, north to Harlem, and finally to the ancient Middle East, where a

man by the name of Herod the Great became the High John of
his time. The arc of the work remains original. The reader returns
from the joy of these writings once again feeling wholly refreshed.

Bob Callahan,
Berkeley, Fall 1984

S · P · U · N · K

S · P · U · N · K

A GIANT OF A brown-skinned man sauntered up the one street of the village and out into the palmetto thickets with a small pretty woman clinging lovingly to his arm.

"Looka theah, folkses!" cried Elijah Mosley, slapping his leg gleefully. "Theah they go, big as life an' brassy as tacks."

All the loungers in the store tried to walk to the door with an air of nonchalance but with small success.

"Now pee-eople!" Walter Thomas gasped. "Will you look at 'em!"

"But that's one thing Ah likes about Spunk Banks—he ain't skeered of nothin' on God's green footstool—*nothin'*! He rides that log down at saw-mill jus' like he struts 'round wid another man's wife—jus' don't give a kitty. When Tes' Miller got cut to giblets on that circle-saw, Spunk steps right up and starts ridin'. The rest of us was skeered to go near it."

A round-shouldered figure in overalls much too large came nervously in the door and the talking ceased. The men looked at each other and winked.

"Gimme some soda-water. Sass'prilla Ah reckon," the newcomer ordered, and stood far down the counter near the open pickled pig-feet tub to drink it.

Elijah nudged Walter and turned with mock gravity to the new-comer.

"Say, Joe, how's everything up yo' way? How's yo' wife?"

Joe started and all but dropped the bottle he was holding. He swallowed several times painfully and his lips trembled.

"Aw 'Lige, you oughtn't to do nothin' like that," Walter grumbled. Elijah ignored him.

"She jus' passed heah a few minutes ago goin' thata way," with a wave of his hand in the direction of the woods.

Now Joe knew his wife had passed that way. He knew that the men lounging in the general store had seen her, moreover, he knew that the men knew *he* knew. He stood there silent for a long moment staring blankly, with his Adam's apple twitching nervously up and down his throat. One could actually *see* the pain he was suffering, his eyes, his face, his hands and even the dejected slump of his shoulders. He set the bottle down upon the counter. He didn't bang it, just eased it out of his hand silently and fiddled with his suspender buckle.

"Well, Ah'm goin' after her to-day. Ah'm goin' an' fetch her back. Spunk's done gone too fur."

He reached deep down into his trouser pocket and drew out a hollow ground razor, large and shiny, and passed his moistened thumb back and forth over the edge.

"Talkin' like a man, Joe. 'Course that's yo' fambly affairs, but Ah like to see grit in anybody."

Joe Kanty laid down a nickel and stumbled out into the street.

Dusk crept in from the woods. Ike Clarke lit the swinging oil lamp that was almost immediately surrounded by candle-flies. The men laughed boisterously behind Joe's back as they watched him shamble woodward.

"You oughtn't to said whut you did to him, Lige—look how it worked him up," Walter chided.

"And Ah hope it did work him up. Tain't even decent for a man to take and take like he do."

"Spunk will sho' kill him."

"Aw, Ah doan know. You never kin tell. He might turn him up an' spank him fur gettin' in the way, but Spunk wouldn't shoot no unarmed man. Dat razor he carried outa heah ain't gonna run Spunk down an' cut him, an' Joe ain't got the nerve to go up to Spunk with it knowing he totes that Army .45. He makes that break outa heah to bluff us. He's gonna hide that razor behind the first palmetto root an' sneak back home to bed. Don't tell me nothin' 'bout that rabbit-foot colored man. Didn't he meet Spunk an' Lena face to face one day las' week an' mumble sumthin' to Spunk 'bout lettin' his wife alone?"

"What did Spunk say?" Walter broke in, "Ah like him fine but tain't right the way he carris on wid Lena Kanty, jus' 'cause Joe's timid 'bout fightin'."

"You wrong theah, Walter. Tain't 'cause Joe's timid at all, it's 'cause Spunk wants Lena. If Joe was a passle of wile cats Spunk would tackle the job just the same. He'd go after *anything* he wanted the same way. As Ah wuz sayin' a minute ago, he tole Joe right to his face that Lena was his. 'Call her and see if she'll come. A woman knows her boss an' she answers when he calls.' 'Lena, ain't I yo' husband?' Joe sorter whines out. Lena looked at him real disgusted but she don't answer and she don't move outa her tracks. Then Spunk reaches out an' takes hold of her arm an' says: 'Lena, youse mine. From now on Ah works for you an' fights for you an' Ah never wants you to look to nobody for a crumb of bread, a stitch of close or a shingle to go over yo' head, but *me* long as Ah live. Ah'll git the lumber foh owah house to-morrow. Go home an' git yo' things together!'

" 'Thass mah house,' Lena speaks up. 'Papa gimme that.'

" 'Well,' says Spunk, 'doan give up whut's yours, but when youse inside doan forgit youse mine, an' let no other man git outa his place wid you!'

"Lena looked up at him with her eyes so full of love that they wuz runnin' over, an' Spunk seen it an' Joe seen it too, and his lip started to tremblin' and his Adam's apple was galloping up and down his neck like a race horse. Ah bet he's wore out half a dozen Adam's apples since Spunk's been on the job with Lena. That's all he'll do. He'll be back heah after while swallowin' an' workin' his lips like he wants to say somethin' an' can't."

"But didn't he do *nothin'* to stop 'em?"

"Nope, not a frazzlin' thing—jus' stood there. Spunk took Lena's arm and walked off jus' like nothin' ain't happened and he stood there gazin' after them till they was outa sight. Now you know a woman don't want no man like that. I'm jus' waitin' to see whut he's goin' to say when he gits back."

II

But Joe Kanty never came back, never. The men in the store heard the sharp report of a pistol somewhere distant in the palmetto thicket and soon Spunk came walking leisurely, with his big black Stetson set at the same rakish angle and Lena clinging to his arm, came walking right into the general store. Lena wept in a frightened manner.

"Well," Spunk announced calmly, "Joe come out there wid a meat axe an' made me kill him."

He sent Lena home and led the men back to Joe — crumpled and limp with his right hand still clutching his razor.

"See mah back? Mah close cut clear through. He sneaked

up an' tried to kill me from the back, but Ah got him, an' got him good, first shot," Spunk said.

The men glared at Elijah, accusingly.

"Take him up an' plant him in Stony Lonesome," Spunk said in a careless voice. "Ah didn't wanna shoot him but he made me do it. He's a dirty coward, jumpin' on a man from behind."

Spunk turned on his heel and sauntered away to where he knew his love wept in fear for him and no man stopped him. At the general store later on, they all talked of locking him up until the sheriff should come from Orlando, but no one did anything but talk.

A clear case of self-defense, the trial was a short one, and Spunk walked out of the court house to freedom again. He could work again, ride the dangerous log-carriage that fed the singing, snarling, biting circle-saw; he could stroll the soft dark lanes with his guitar. He was free to roam the woods again; he was free to return to Lena. He did all of these things.

III

"Whut you reckon, Walt?" Elijah asked one night later. "Spunk's gittin' ready to marry Lena!"

"Naw! Why, Joe ain't had time to git cold yit. Nohow Ah didn't figger Spunk was the marryin' kind."

"Well, he is," rejoined Elijah. "He done moved most of Lena's things — and her along wid 'em — over to the Bradley house. He's buying it. Jus' like Ah told yo' all right in heah the night Joe wuz kilt. Spunk's crazy 'bout Lena. He don't want folks to keep on talkin' 'bout her — thass reason he's rushin' so. Funny thing 'bout that bob-cat, wan't it?"

"What bob-cat, 'Lige? Ah ain't heered 'bout none."

"Ain't cher? Well, night befo' las' as they was goin' to bed, a big black bob-cat, black all over, you hear me, *black*, walked round and round that house and howled like forty, an' when Spunk got his gun an' went to the winder to shoot it, he says it stood right still an' looked him in the eye, an' howled right at him. The thing got Spunk so nervoused up he couldn't shoot. But Spunk says twan't no bob-cat nohow. He says it was Joe done sneaked back from Hell!"

"Humph!" sniffed Walter, "he oughter be nervous after what he done. Ah reckon Joe come back to dare him to marry Lena, or to come out an' fight. Ah bet he'll be back time and again, too. Know what Ah think? Joe wuz a braver man than Spunk."

There was a general shout of derision from the group.

"Thass a fact," went on Walter. "Lookit whut he done; took a razor an' went out to fight a man he knowed toted a gun an' wuz a crack shot, too; 'nother thing Joe wuz skeered of Spunk, skeered plumb stiff! But he went jes' the same. It took him a long time to get his nerve up. Tain't nothin' for Spunk to fight when he ain't skeered of nothin'. Now, Joe's done come back to have it out wid the man that's got all he ever had. Y'all know Joe ain't never had nothin' nor wanted nothin' besides Lena. It musta been a h'ant cause ain't nobody never seen no black bob-cat."

" 'Nother thing," cut in one of the men, "Spunk wuz cussin' a blue streak to-day 'cause he 'lowed dat saw wuz wobblin' — almos' got 'im once. The machinist come, looked it over an' said it wuz alright. Spunk musta been leanin' t'wards it some. Den he claimed somebody pushed 'im but twan't nobody close to 'im. Ah wuz glad when knockin' off time come. I'm skeered of dat man when he gits hot. He'd beat you full of button holes as quick as he's look atcher."

IV

The men gathered the next evening in a different mood, no laughter. No badinage this time.

"Look, 'Lige, you goin' to set up wid Spunk?"

"Naw, Ah reckon not, Walter. Tell yuh the truth, Ah'm a li'l bit skittish. Spunk died too wicket—died cussin' he did. You know he thought he was done outa life."

"Good Lawd, who'd he think done it?"

"Joe."

"Joe Kanty? How come?"

"Walter, Ah b'leeve Ah will walk up thata way an' set. Lena would like it Ah reckon."

"But whut did he say, 'Lige?"

Elijah did not answer until they had left the lighted store and were strolling down the dark street.

"Ah wuz loadin' a wagon wid scantlin' right near the saw when Spunk fell on the carriage but 'fore Ah could git to him the saw got him in the body—awful sight. Me an' Skint Miller got him off but it was too late. Anybody could see that. The fust thing he said wuz: 'He pushed me, 'Lige—the dirty hound pushed me in the back!'—he was spittin' blood at ev'ry breath. We laid him on the sawdust pile with his face to the East so's he could die easy. He helt mah han' till the last, Walter, and said: 'It was Joe, 'Lige . . . the dirty sneak shoved me . . . he didn't dare come to mah face . . . but Ah'll git the son-of-a-wood louse soon's Ah get there an' make hell too hot for him . . . Ah felt him shove me . . . !' Thass how he died."

"If spirits kin fight, there's a powerful tussle goin' on some-where ovah Jordan 'cause Ah b'leeve Joe's ready for Spunk an' ain't skeered any more—yas, Ah b'leeve Joe pushed 'im mah-self."

They had arrived at the house. Lena's lamentations were deep and loud. She had filled the room with magnolia blossoms that gave off a heavy sweet odor. The keepers of the wake tipped about whispering in frightened tones. Everyone in the village was there, even old Jeff Kanty, Joe's father, who a few hours before would have been afraid to come within ten feet of him, stood leering triumphantly down upon the fallen giant as if his fingers had been the teeth of steel that laid him low.

The cooling board consisted of three sixteen-inch boards on saw horses, a dingy sheet was his shroud.

The women ate heartily of the funeral baked meats and wondered who would be Lena's next. The men whispered coarse conjectures between guzzles of whiskey.

"YOU ISIE WATTS! Git 'own offen dat gate post an' rake up dis yahd!"

The small brown girl perched upon the gate post looked yearningly up the gleaming shell road that lead to Orlando. After awhile, she shrugged her thin shoulders. This only seemed to heap still more kindling on Grandma Potts' already burning ire.

"Lawd a-mussy!" she screamed, enraged—"Heah Joel, gimme dat wash stick. Ah'll show dat limb of Satan she cain't shake herself at *me*. If she ain't down by the time Ah gets dere, Ah'll break huh down in de lines."

"Aw Gran'ma, Ah see Mist' George and Jim Robinson comin' and Ah wanted to wave at 'em," the child said impatiently.

"You jes' wave dat rake at dis heah yahd, madame, else Ah'll take you down a button hole lower. Youse too 'oomanish jumpin' up in everybody's face dat pass."

This struck the child sorely for nothing pleased her so much as to sit atop of the gate post and hail the passing vehicles on their way South to Orlando, or North to Sanford. That white shell road was her great attraction. She raced up and down the stretch of it that lay before her gate like a round-eyed puppy hailing gleefully all travelers. Everybody in the country, white and colored, knew little Isis Watts, Isis the Joyful. The Robinson brothers, white cattlemen, were particularly fond of her and always extended a stirrup for her to climb up behind one of them for a short ride, or let her try to crack the long bull whips and *yee whoo* at the cows.

Grandma Potts went inside and Isis literally waved the rake at the 'chaws' of ribbon cane that lay so bountifully about the yard in company with the knots and peelings, with a thick sprinkling of peanut hulls.

The herd of cattle in their envelope of gray dust came alongside and Isis dashed out to the nearest stirrup and was lifted up.

"Hello theah Snidlits, I was wonderin' wheah you was," said Jim Robinson as she snuggled down behind him in the saddle. They were almost out of the danger zone when Grandma emerged. "You Isie," she bawled.

The child slid down on the opposite side of the house and executed a flank movement through the corn patch that brought her into the yard from behind the privy.

"You li'l hasion you! Wheah you been?"

"Out in de back yahd," Isis lied and did a cart wheel and a few fancy steps on her way to the front again.

"If you doan git in dat yahd, Ah make a mommuk of you!" Isis observed that Grandma was cutting a fancy assortment of switches from peach, guana and cherry trees.

She finished the yard by raking everything under the edge of the porch and began a romp with the dogs, those lean, floppy-eared hounds that all country folks keep. But Grandma vetoed this also.

"Isie, you set on dat porch! Uh great big 'leben yeah ole gal racin' an' rompin' lak dat — set 'own!'"

Isis flung herself upon the steps.

"Git up offa dem steps, you aggravatin' limb, 'fore Ah git dem hick'ries tuh you, an' set yo' seff on a cheah."

Isis arose, and then sat down as violently as possible in the chair. She slid down, and down, until she all but sat on her own shoulder blades.

"Now look atcher," Grandma screamed, "Put yo' knees together, an' git up offen yo' backbone! Lawd, you know dis hellion is gwine make me stomp huh insides out."

Isis sat bolt upright as if she wore a ramrod down her back and began to whistle. Now there are certain things that Grandma Potts felt no one of this female persuasion should do — one was to sit with the knees separated, 'settin' brazen' she called it; another was whistling, another playing with boys. Finally, a lady must never cross her legs.

Grandma jumped up from her seat to get the switches.

"So youse whistlin' in mah face, huh!" She glared till her eyes were beady and Isis bolted for safety. But the noon hour brought John Watts the widowed father, and this excused the child from sitting for criticism.

Being the only girl in the family, of course she must wash the dishes, which she did in intervals between frolics with the dogs. She even gave Jake, the puppy, a swim in the dishpan by holding him suspended above the water that reeked of 'pot likker' — just high enough so that his feet would be immersed. The deluded puppy swam and swam without ever crossing the pan, much to his annoyance. Hearing Grandma she hurriedly dropped him on the floor, which he tracked-up with feet wet with dishwater.

Grandma took her patching and settled down in the front

room to sew. She did this every afternoon, and invariably slept in the big red rocker with her head lolled back over the back, the sewing falling from her hand.

Isis had crawled under the center table with its red plush cover with little round balls for fringe. She was lying on her back imagining herself various personages. She wore trailing robes, golden slippers with blue bottoms. She rode white horses with flaring pink nostrils to the horizon, for she still believed that to be land's end. She was picturing herself gazing over the edge of the world into the abyss when the spool of cotton fell from Grandma's lap and rolled away under the whatnot. Isis drew back from her contemplation of the nothingness at the horizon and glanced up at the sleeping woman. Her head had fallen far back. She breathed with a regular 'mark' intake and 'poosah' exhaust. But Isis was a visual-minded child. She heard the snores only subconsciously but she saw the straggling beard on Grandma's chin, trembling a little with every 'mark' and 'poosah'. They were long gray hairs curled every here and there against the dark brown skin. Isis was moved with pity for her mother's mother.

"Poah Gran-ma needs a shave," she murmured, and set about it. Just then Joel, next older than Isis, entered with a can of bait.

"Come on Isie, les' we all go fishin'. The Perch is bitin' fine in Blue Sink."

"Sh-sh—" cautioned his sister, "Ah got to shave Gran'ma."

"Who say so?" Joel asked, surprised.

"Nobody doan hafta tell me. Look at her chin. No ladies don't weah whiskers if they kin help it. But Gran-ma gittin ole an' she doan know how to shave lak *me*."

The conference adjourned to the back porch lest Grandma wake.

"Aw, Isie, you doan know nothin' 'bout shavin' a-tall—but a *man* lak *me*—"

"Ah do so know."

"You don't not. Ah'm goin' shave her mahseff."

"Naw, you won't neither, Smarty. Ah saw her first an' thought it all up first," Isis declared, and ran to the calico-covered box on the wall above the wash basin and seized her father's razor. Joel was quick and seized the mug and brush.

"Now!" Isis cried defiantly, "Ah got the razor."

"Goody, goody, goody, pussy cat, Ah got th' brush an' you can't shave 'thout lather—see! Ah know mo' than you," Joel retorted.

"Aw, who don't know dat?" Isis pretended to scorn. But seeing her progress blocked from lack of lather she compromised.

"Ah know! Les' we all shave her. You lather an' Ah shave."

This was agreeable to Joel. He made mountains of lather and anointed his own chin, and the chin of Isis and the dogs, splashed the wall and at last was persuaded to lather Grandma's chin. Not that he was loath but he wanted his new plaything to last as long as possible.

Isis stood on one side of the chair with the razor clutched cleaver fashion. The niceties of razor-handling had passed over her head. The thing with her was to *hold* the razor—sufficient in itself.

Joel splashed on the lather in great gobs and Grandma awoke.

For one bewildered moment she stared at the grinning boy with the brush and mug but sensing another presence, she turned to behold the business face of Isis and the razor-clutching hand. Her jaw dropped and Grandma, forgetting years and rheumatism, bolted from the chair and fled the house, screaming.

"She's gone to tell papa, Isie. You didn't have no business wid his razor and he's gonna lick yo' hide," Joel cried, running to replace mug and brush.

"You too, chuckle-head, you too," retorted Isis. "You was playin' wid his brush and put it all over the dogs — Ah seen you put in on Ned an' Beulah." Isis shaved and replaced it in the box. Joel took his bait and pole and hurried to Blue Sink. Isis crawled under the house to brood over the whipping she knew would come. She had meant well.

But sounding brass and tinkling cymbal drew her forth. The local lodge of the Grand United Order of Odd Fellows, led by a braying, thudding band, was marching in full regalia down the road. She had forgotten the barbecue and log-rolling to be held today for the benefit of the new hall.

Music to Isis meant motion. In a minute razor and whipping forgotten, she was doing a fair imitation of a Spanish dancer she had seen in a medicine show some time before. Isis' feet were gifted — she could dance most anything she saw.

Up, up, went her spirits, her small feet doing all sorts of intricate things and her body in rhythm, hand curving above her head. But the music was growing faint. Grandma was nowhere in sight. Isis stole out of the gate, running and dancing after the band.

Not far down the road, Isis stopped. She realized she couldn't dance at the carnival. Her dress was torn and dirty. She picked a long-stemmed daisy, and placed it behind her ear, but her dress remained torn and dirty just the same. Then Isis had an idea. Her thoughts returned to the battered, round-topped trunk back in the bedroom. She raced back to the house; then, happier, she raced down the white dusty road to the picnic grove, gorgeously clad. People laughed good-naturedly at her, the band played and Isis danced because she couldn't help it. A crowd of children gathered admiringly about her as she wheeled lightly about, hand on hip, flower between her teeth with the red and white fringe of the tablecloth—Grandma's new red tablecloth that she wore in lieu of a Spanish shawl—trailing in the dust. It was too ample for her meager form, but she wore it like a gypsy. Her brown feet twinkled in and out of the fringe. Some grown people joined the children about her. The Grand Exalted Ruler rose to speak; the band was hushed, but Isis danced on, the crowd clapping their hands for her. No one listened to the Exalted one, for little by little the multitude had surrounded the small brown dancer.

An automobile drove up to the Crown and halted. Two white men and a lady got out and pushed into the crowd, suppressing mirth discretely behind gloved hands. Isis looked up and waved them a magnificent hail and went on dancing until—

Grandma had returned to the house, and missed Isis. She straightaway sought her at the festivities, expecting to find her in her soiled dress, shoeless, standing at the far edge of the crowd. What she saw now drove her frantic. Here was her granddaughter dancing before a gaping crowd in her brand new red tablecloth, and reeking of lemon extract. Isis had added the final touch to her costume. Of course she must also have perfume.

When Isis saw her Grandma, she bolted. She heard her Grandma cry—"Mah Gawd, mah brand new tablecloth Ah just bought f'um O'landah!"—as Isis fled through the crowd and on into the woods.

Isis followed the little creek until she came to the ford in a rutty wagon road that led to Apopka and laid down on the cool grass at the roadside. The April sun was quite warm.

Misery, misery and woe settled down upon her. The child wept. She knew another whipping was in store.

"Oh, Ah wish Ah could die, then Gran'ma an' papa would be sorry they beat me so much. Ah b'leeve Ah'll run away and never go home no mo'. Ah'm goin' drown mahseff in th' creek!"

Isis got up and waded into the water. She routed out a tiny 'gator and a huge bullfrog. She splashed and sang. Soon she was enjoying herself immensely. The purr of a motor struck her ear and she saw a large, powerful car jolting along the rutty road toward her. It stopped at the water's edge.

"Well, I declare, it's our little gypsy," exclaimed the man at the wheel. "What are you doing here, now?"

"Ah'm killin' mahseff," Isis declared dramatically, "Cause Gran'ma beats me too much."

There was a hearty burst of laughter from the machine.

"You'll last some time the way you are going about it. Is this the way to Maitland? We want to go to the Park Hotel."

Isis saw no longer any reason to die. She came up out of the water, holding up the dripping fringe of the tablecloth.

"Naw, indeedy. You go to Maitlan' by the shell road—it goes by mah house—an' turn off at Lake Sebelia to the clay road that takes you right to the do'."

"Well," went on the driver, smiling furtively, "Could you quit dying long enough to go with us?"

"Yessuh," she said thoughtfully, "Ah wanta go wid you."

The door of the car swung open. She was invited to a seat beside the driver. She had often dreamed of riding in one of these heavenly chariots but never thought she would, actually.

"Jump in then, Madame Tragedy, and show us. We lost ourselves after we left your barbecue."

During the drive Isis explained to the kind lady who smelt

faintly of violets and to the indifferent men that she was really a princess. She told them about her trips to the horizon, about the trailing gowns, the gold shoes with blue bottoms — she insisted on the blue bottoms — the white charger, the time when she was Hercules and had slain numerous dragons and sundry giants. At last the car approached her gate over which stood the umbrella chinaberry tree. The car was abreast of the gate and had all but passed when Grandma spied her glorious tablecloth lying back against the upholstery of the Packard.

"You Isie-e!" she bawled, "You li'l wretch you! Come heah *dis instant.*"

"That's me," the child confessed, mortified, to the lady on the rear seat.

"Oh Sewell, stop the car. This is where the child lives. I hate to give her up though."

"Do you wanta keep me?" Isis brightened.

"Oh, I wish I could. Wait, I'll try to save you a whipping this time."

She dismounted with the gaudy lemon-flavored culprit and advanced to the gate where Grandma stood glowering, switches in hand.

"You're gointuh ketchit f'um yo' haid to yo' heels m'lady. Jes' come in heah."

"Why, good afternoon," she accosted the furious grandparent. "You're not going to whip this poor little thing, are you?" the lady asked in conciliatory tones.

"Yes, Ma'am. She's de wustest li'l limb dat ever drawed bref. Jes' look at mah new tablecloth, dat ain't never been washed. She done traipsed all over de woods, uh dancin' an' uh prancin' in it. She done took a razor to me t'day an' Lawd knows whut mo'."

Isis clung to the stranger's hand fearfully.

"Ah wuzn't gointer hurt Gran'ma, miss — Ah wuz just gointer shave her whiskers fuh huh 'cause she's old an' can't."

·The white hand closed tightly over the little brown one that
was quite soiled. She could understand a voluntary act of love
even though it miscarried.

"Now, Mrs. er-er-I didn't get the name — how much did
your tablecloth cost?"

"One whole big silvah dollar down at O'landah — ain't had
it a week yit."

"Now here's five dollars to get another one. I want her to go
to the hotel and dance for me. I could stand a little light
today — "

"Oh, yessum, yessum," Grandma cut in, "Everything's alright, sho' she kin go, yessum."

Feeling that Grandma had been somewhat squelched did
not detract from Isis' spirit at all. She pranced over to the
waiting motor-car and this time seated herself on the rear seat
between the sweet-smiling lady and the rather aloof man in
gray.

"Ah'm gointer stay wid you all," she said with a great deal
of warmth, and snuggled up to her benefactress. "Want me tuh
sing a song fuh you?"

"There, Helen, you've been adopted," said the man with a
short, harsh laugh.

"Oh, I hope so, Harry." She put her arm about the red-
draped figure at her side and drew it close until she felt the
warm puffs of the child's breath against her side. She looked
hungrily ahead of her and spoke into space rather than to
anyone in the car. "I would like just a little of her sunshine to
soak into my soul. I would like that alot."

M · U · T · T · S · Y

THE PIANO IN Ma Turner's back parlor stuttered and wailed. The pianist kept time with his heel and informed an imaginary deserter that "she might leave and go to Halimufack, but his slow-drag would bring her back," mournfully, with a memory of tom-toms running rhythm through the plaint.

Fewclothes burst through the portieres, a brown chrysalis from a dingy red cocoon, and touched the player on the shoulder.

"Say, Muttsy," he stage whispered, "Ma's got a new li'l biddy in there—just come. And say—her foot would make all of dese Harlem babies a Sunday face."

"Whut she look like?" Muttsy drawled trying to maintain his characteristic pose of near indifference to the female sex.

"Brown skin, patent leather grass on her knob, kinder tallish. She's a li'l skinny," he added apologetically, "but Ah'm willing to buy corn for that li'l chicken."

Muttsy lifted his six feet from the piano bench as slowly as his curiosity would let him and sauntered to the portieres for a peep. The sight was as pleasing as Fewclothes had stated only more so. He went on in the room which Ma always kept empty.

It was her receiving room — her 'front'.

From Ma's manner it was evident that she was very glad to see the girl. She could see that the girl was not overjoyed in her presence, but she attributed that to southern greenness.

"Who you say sentcher heah, dearie?" Ma asked, her face trying to beam, but looking harder and more forbidding.

"Uh-a-a man down at the boat landing where I got off — North River. I jus' come in on the boat."

Ma's husband from his corner spoke up.

"Musta been Bluefront."

"Yeah, musta been him," Muttsy agreed.

"Oh, it's all right, honey, we New Yorkers likes to know who we'se takin' in, dearie. We has to be keerful. Whut did you say yo' name was?"

"Pinkie, mam, Pinkie Jones."

Ma stared hard at the little old battered reticule that the girl carried for luggage — not many clothes if that was all, she reflected. But Pinkie had everything she needed in her face — many, many trunks full. Several of them for Ma. She noticed the cold-reddened knuckles of her bare hands too.

"Come on upstairs to yo' room — thass all right 'bout the price — we'll come to some 'greement tomorrow. Jes' go up and take off yo' things."

Pinkie put back the little rusty leather purse of another generation and followed Ma. She didn't like Ma — her smile resembled the smile of the Wolf in *Red Riding Hood*. Anyway back in Eatonville, Florida, 'ladies', especially old ones, didn't put powder and paint on their faces.

"Forty-dollars-Kate sure landed a pippin' dis time," said Muttsy, *sotto voce*, to Fewclothes back at the piano, "If she ain't, then there ain't a hound dawk in Georgy. Ah'm goin' home an' dress."

No one else in the crowded back parlor let alone the house knew of Pinkie's coming. They danced on, played on, sang their blues and lived on hotly their intense lives. The two men who had seen her — no one counted old man Turner — went on playing too, but kept an ear cocked for her coming.

She followed Ma downstairs and seated herself in the parlor with the old man. He sat in a big rocker before a copper-lined gas stove, indolence in every gesture.

"Ah'm Ma's husband," he announced by way of making conversation.

"Now you jus' shut up!" Ma commanded severely. "You gointer git yo' teeth knocked down yo' throat for runnin' yo' tongue. Lemme talk to dis gal — dis is *mah* house. You sets on the stool un do nothin' too much tuh have anything tuh talk over!"

"Oh, Lawd," groaned the old man feeling a knee that always pained him at the mention of work. "Oh, Lawd, will you sen' yo' fiery chariot an' take me 'way from heah?"

"Aw shet up!" the woman spit out. "Lawd don't wantcher — devil wouldn't have yuh." She peered into the girl's face and leaned back satisfied.

"Well, girlie, you kin be a lotta help tuh me 'round dis house if you takes un intrus' in things — oh Lawd!" She leapt up from her seat. "That's mah bread ah smell burnin' . . . "

No sooner had Ma's feet cleared the room than the old man came to life again. He peered furtively after the broad back of his wife.

"Know who she is?" he asked Pinkie in an awed whisper. She shook her head. "You don't? Dat's Forty-dollars-Kate!"

"Forty-dollars-Kate?" Pinkie repeated open-eyed. "Naw, I don't know nothin' 'bout her."

"Sh-h," cautioned the old man. "Course you don't. I fuhgits

you ain't nothin' 'tall but a young'un. Twenty-five years ago they all called her dat 'cause she *wuz* 'Forty-dollars-Kate.' She sho' wuz some p'utty 'oman—great big robus' lookin' gal. Men wuz glad 'nough to spend forty dollars on her if dey had it. She didn't lose no time wid dem dat didn't have it."

He grinned ingratiatingly at Pinkie and leaned nearer.

"But youse better lookin' than she ever wuz, you might— tain't no tellin' whut you might do ef you gat some sense. I'm gointer teach you, hear?"

"Yessuh," the girl managed to answer with an almost paralyzed tongue.

"Thass a good girl. You jus' lissen to me an' you'll pull thew alright."

He glanced at the girl sitting timidly upon the edge of the chair and scolded.

"Don't set dataway," he ejaculated. "Yo' backbone ain't no ramrod. Kinda scooch down on the for'ard edge uh de chear lak dis." (He demonstrated by 'scooching' forward so far that he was almost sitting on his shoulder-blades.) The girl slumped a little.

"Is you got a job yit?"

"Nawsuh," she answered slowly, "but I reckon I'll have one soon. Ain't been in town a day yet."

"You looks kinda young—kinda little biddy. Is you been to school much?"

"Yessuh, went thew eighth reader. I'm goin' again when I get a chance."

"Dat so? Well ah reckon ah kin talk some Latin tuh yuh den." He cleared his throat loudly. "Whut's you entitlum?"

"I don't know," said the girl in confusion.

"Well, den, whut's you entrimmins," he querried with a bit of braggadocia in his voice.

"I don't know," from the girl, after a long awkward pause.

"You chillin don't learn nothin' in school these days. Is you got to 'goes into' yit?"

"You mean long division?"

"Ain't askin' 'bout de longness of it, dat don't make no difference," he retorted, "Sence you goin' stay heah ah'll edgecate yuh — do yuh know how to eat a fish — uh nice brown fried fish?"

"Yessuh," she answered quickly, looking about for the fish. "How?"

"Why, you jus' eat it with corn bread," she said, a bit disappointed at the non-appearance of the fish.

"Well, ah'll tell yuh," he patronized. "You starts at de tail and liffs off de bones sorter gentle and eats him clear tuh de head on dat side; den you turn 'im ovah an' commence at de tail agin and eat right up tuh de head; den you push *dem* bones way tuh one side an' takes another fish an' so on 'till de end — well, 'till der ain't no mo'!"

He mentally digested the fish and went on. "See," he pointed accusingly at her feet, "you don't even know how tuh warm yoself! You settin' dere wid yo' feet ev'y which way. Dat ain't de way tuh git wahm. Now look at *mah* feet. Dass right put bofe big toes right tegethah — now shove 'em close up tuh de fiah; now lean back so! Dass de way. Ah knows uh heap uh things tuh teach yuh sense you gointer live heah — ah learns all of 'em while de ole lady is paddlin' roun' out dere in de yard."

Ma appeared at the door and the old man withdrew so far into his rags that he all but disappeared. They went to supper where there was fried fish but forgot all rules for eating it and just ate heartily. She helped with the dishes and returned to the parlor. A little later some more men and women knocked and were admitted after the same furtive peering out through the nearest crack of the door. Ma carried them all back to the kitchen and Pinkie heard the clink of glasses and much loud laughter. Women came in by ones and twos, some in shabby coats turned up about the ears, and with various cheap but showy hats crushed down over unkempt hair. More men, more women, more trips to the kitchen with loud laughter.

Pinkie grew uneasy. Both men and women stared at her. She kept strictly to her place. Ma came in and tried to make her join the others.

"Come on in, honey, a li'l toddy ain't gointer hurt nobody. Evebody knows *me*, ah wouldn't touch a hair on yo' head. Come on in, dearie, all th' men wants tuh meetcher."

Pinkie smelt the liquor on Ma's breath and felt contaminated at her touch. She wished herself back home again even with the ill treatment and squalor. She thought of the three dollars she had secreted in her shoe — she had been warned against pick-pockets — and flight but where? Nowhere. For there was no home to which *she* could return, nor any place else she knew of. But when she got a job, she'd scrape herself clear of people who took toddies.

A very black man sat on the piano stool playing as only a Negro can, stamping with his feet, and the rest of his body keeping time —

> *Ahm gointer make me a graveyard of mah own*
> *Ahm gointer make me a graveyard of mah own*
> *Carried me down on de Smoky Road—*

Pinkie, weary of Ma's maudlin coaxing caught these lines as she was being pulled and coaxed into the kitchen. Everyone in there was shaking shimmies to music, rolling eyes heavenward as they picked imaginary grapes out of the air. "Folkses," shouted Ma, "Look a-heah! Shut up dis racket! Ah wantcher tuh meet Pinkie Jones. She's de bes' frien' ah got." Ma flopped into a chair and began to cry into her whiskey glass.

"Mah comperments!" The men almost shouted. The women were less, much less enthusiastic.

"Dass de las' run uh shad," laughed a woman called Ada, pointing to Pinkie's slenderness.

"Jes' lak a bar uh soap aftah uh hard week's wash," Bertha chimed in and laughed uproariously. The men didn't help.

"Oh, Miss Pinkie," said Bluefront, removing his Stetson for the first time, "Ma'am, also Ma'am, ef you wuz tuh see me settin' straddle of uh Mudcat leadin' a minner whut ud you think?"

"I-er, oh, I don't know, suh. I didn't know you-er anybody could ride uh fish."

"Stick uh roun' me, baby, an' you'll wear diamon's." Bluefront swaggered. "Look heah, li'l Pigmeat, youse *some* sharp! If you didn't had but one eye ah'd think you wuz a needle — thass how sharp you looks to me. Say, mah right foot is itchin'. Do dat mean ah'm gointer walk on some strange ground wid you?"

"Naw, indeedy," cut in Fewclothes. "It jes' means you feet needs to walk in some strange water — wid a li'l read seal lye thowed in."

But he was not to have a monopoly. Fewclothes and Shorty joined the chase and poor Pinkie found it impossible to retreat to her place beside the old man. She hung her head, embarrassed that she did not understand their mode of speech; she felt the unfriendly eyes of the women, and she loathed the smell of liquor that filled the house now. The piano still rumbled and wailed that same song —

Carried me down on de Smoky Road
Brought me back on de coolin' board
Ahm gointer make me a graveyard of mah own.

A surge of cold, fresh air from the outside stirred the smoke and liquor fumes and Pinkie knew that the front door was open. She turned her eyes that way and thought of flight to the clean outside. The door stood wide open and a tall figure in an overcoat with a fur collar stood there.

"Good Gawd, Muttsy! Shet 'at do'," cried Shorty. "Dass a pure razor blowing out dere tonight. Ah didn't know you wuz outa here nohow."

Carried me down on de Smoky Road
Brought me back on de coolin' board
Ahm gointer make me a graveyard of mah own,

sang Muttsy, looking as if he sought someone and banged the door shut on the last words. He strode on in without removing hat or coat.

Pinkie saw in this short space that all the men deferred to him, that all the women sought his notice. She tried timidly to squeeze between two of the men and return to the quiet place beside old man Turner, thinking that Muttsy would hold the attention of her captors until she had escaped. But Muttsy spied her through the men about her and joined them. By this time her exasperation and embarrassment had her on the point of tears.

"Well, whadda yuh know about dis!" he exclaimed, "A real li'l pullet."

"Look out dere, Muttsy," drawled Dramsleg with objection, catching Pinkie by the arm and trying to draw her toward him. "Lemme tell dis li'l Pink Mama how crazy ah is 'bout her mahself. Ah ain't got no lady atall an' — "

"Aw shut up Drams," Muttsy said sternly, "put yo' pocket-book where yo' mouf' is, an' somebody will lissen. Ah'm a heavy-sugar papa. Ah eats fried chicken when the rest of you niggers is drinking rain-water."

He thrust some of the others aside and stood squarely before her. With her downcast eyes, she saw his well-polished shoes, creased trousers, gloved hands and at last timidly raised her eyes to his face.

"Look a heah!" he frowned, "you roughnecks done got dis baby ready tuh cry."

He put his forefinger under her chin and made her look at him. And for some reason he removed his hat.

"Come on in the sittin' room an' le's talk. Come on befo' some uh dese niggers sprinkle some salt on yuh and eat yuh clean up lak uh raddish." Dramsleg looked after Muttsy and the girl as they swam through the smoke into the front room. He beckoned to Bluefront.

"Hey, Bluefront! Ain't you mah frien'?"

"Yep," answered Bluefront.

"Well, then why cain't you help me? Muttsy done me dirt wid the li'l pig-meat — throw a louse on 'im."

Pinkie's hair was slippin' down. She felt it, but her self-consciousness prevented her from catching it and down it fell in a heavy roll that spread out and covered her nearly to the waist. She followed Muttsy into the front room and again sat shrinking in the corner. She did not wish to talk to Muttsy nor anyone else in that house, but there were fewer people in this room.

"Phew!" cried Bluefront, "dat baby sho got some righteous moss on her keg — dass reg'lar 'nearrow mah Gawd tuh thee' stuff." He made a lengthy gesture with his arms as if combing out long, silky hair.

"Shux," sneered Ada in a moist, alcoholic voice. "Dat ain't nothin' mah haih useter be so's ah could set on it."

There was general laughter from the men.

"Yas, ah know it's de truth!" shouted Shorty. "It's jes' ez close tuh yo' head *now* ez ninety-nine is tuh uh hund'ed."

"Ah'll call Muttsy tuh you," Ada threatened.

"Oh, 'oman, Muttsy ain't got you tuh study 'bout no mo' 'cause he's parkin' his heart wid dat li'l chicken wid white-folks haih. Why, dat li'l chicken's foot would make you a Sunday face."

General laughter again. Ada dashed the whiskey glass upon the floor with the determined stalk of an angry tiger and arose and started forward.

"Muttsy Owens, uh nobody else ain't to gointer make no fool outer *me*. Dat li'l kack girl ain't gointer put *me* on de bricks — not much."

Perhaps Muttsy heard her, perhaps he saw her out of the corner of his eye and read her mood. But knowing the woman as he did he might have known what she would do under such circumstances. At any rate he got to his feet as she entered the room where he sat with Pinkie.

"Ah know you ain't lost yo' head sho' 'nuff, 'oman. 'Deed, Gawd knows you bettah go 'way f'um me." He said this in a low, steady voice. The music stopped, the talking stopped and even the drinkers paused. Nothing happened, for Ada looked straight into Muttsy's eyes and went on outside.

"Miss Pinkie, Ah votes you g'wan tuh bed," Muttsy said suddenly to the girl.

"Yes-suh."

"An' don't you worry 'bout no job. Ah knows where you kin

git a good one. Ah'll go see 'em first an' tell yuh tomorrow night."

She went off to bed upstairs. The rich baritone of the piano player came up to her as did laughter and shouting. But she was tired and slept soundly.

Ma shuffled in after eight the next morning. "Darlin', ain't you got 'nuff sleep yit?"

Pinkie opened her eyes a trifle. "Ain't you the puttiest li'l trick! An' Muttsy done gone crazy 'bout yuh! Chile, he's lousy wid money an' diamon's an' everything — yuh better grab him quick. Some folks has all de luck. Heah ah is — got uh man dat hates work lak de devil hates holy water. Ah gotta make dis house pay!"

Pinkie's eyes opened wide. "What does Mr. Muttsy do?"

"Mah Gawd, chile! He's de bes' gambler in three states, cards, craps, un hawses. He could be a boss stevedore if he so wanted. The big boss down on de dock would give him a fat job — just begs him to take it 'cause he can manage the men. He's the biggest hero they got since Harry Wills left the waterfront. But he won't take it 'cause he makes so much wid the games."

"He's awful good-lookin'," Pinkie agreed, "an' he been mighty nice tuh me — but I like men to work. I wish he would. Gamblin' ain't nice."

"Yeah, 'tis, ef you makes money lak Muttsy. Maybe yo ain't noticed dat diamon' set in his tooth. He picks women up when he wants tuh an' puts 'em down when he choose."

Pinkie turned her face to the wall and shuddered. Ma paid no attention.

"You doan hafta git up till you git good an' ready, Muttsy says. Ah mean you kin stay roun' the house 'till you come to, sorter."

The day passed. Darkness woke up the land east of Lenox —
all that land between the railroad tracks and the river. Ugly by
day, night kindly hid some of its sordid homeliness. Yes,
nighttime gave it life.

The same women, or others just like them, came to Ma
Turner's. The same men, or men just like them, came as well,
and treated them to liquor, or mistreated them with fists or
cruel jibes. Ma got half drunk as usual and cried over everyone
who would let her.

Muttsy came alone and went straight to Pinkie where she
sat trying to shrink into the wall. She had feared that he would
not come.

"Howdy do, Miss Pinkie."

"How'do do, Mistah Owens," she actually achieved a smile.
"Did you see 'bout m'job?"

"Well, yeah — but the lady says she won't needya fuh uh
week yet. Doan' worry. Ma ain't gointer push yuh foh room
rent. Mah wrist ain't got no cramps.

Pinkie half sobbed: "Ah wantsa job now!"

"Didn't ah say dass alright? Well, Muttsy doan lie. Ah might
jes' es well tell yuh — ahm crazy 'bout yuh — money no objeck."

It was the girl herself who first mentioned 'bed' this night.
He suffered her to go without protest.

The next night she did not come into the sitting room. She
went to bed as soon as the dinner things had been cleared. Ma
begged and cried, but Pinkie pretended illness and kept to her
bed. This she repeated the next night and the next. Every night
Muttsy came and every night he added to his sartorial splendor;
but each night he went away, disappointed, more evidently
crestfallen than before.

But the insistence for escape from her strange surroundings
grew on the girl. When Ma was busy elsewhere, she would take

out the three one-dollar bills from her shoe and reconsider her limitations. If that job would only come on! She felt shut in, imprisoned, walled-in with these women who talked of nothing but men and the numbers and drink, and of men who talked of nothing but the numbers and drink and women. Desperation took her.

One night she was still waiting for the job — Ma's alcoholic tears prevailed. Pinkie took a drink. She drank the stuff mixed with sugar and water and crept to bed even as the dizziness came on. She would not wake tonight. Tomorrow, maybe, the job would come and freedom.

The piano thumped but Pinkie did not hear; the shouts, laughter and cries did not reach her that night. Downstairs Muttsy pushed Ma into a corner.

"Looky heah, Ma. Dat girl done played me long enough. Ah pays her room rent, ah pays her boahd an' all ah gets is uh hunk of ice. Now you said you wuz gointer fix things — you tole me so las' night an heah she done gone tuh bed on me again."

"Deed, ah cain't do nothin' wid huh. She's thinkin' sho' nuff you goin' git her uh job and she fret so 'cause tain't come, dat she drunk uh toddy un hits knocked her down jes' lak uh log."

"Ada an' all uh them laffin' — they say ah done crapped." He felt injured. "Cain't ah go talk to her?"

"Lawdy, Muttsy, dat gal dead drunk an' sleepin' lak she's buried."

"Well, cain't ah go up an' — an' speak tuh her jus' the same?" A yellow-backed bill from Muttsy's roll found itself in Ma's hand and put her in such good humor that she let old man Turner talk all he wanted for the rest of the night.

"Yas, Muttsy, gwan in. Youse *mah* frien'."

Muttsy hurried up to the room indicated. He felt shaky inside there with Pinkie, somehow, but he approached the bed and stood for awhile looking down upon her. Her hair in confusion about her face and swinging off the bedside; the brown arms revealed and the soft lips. He blew out the match he had struck and kissed her full in the mouth, kissed her several times and passed his hand over her neck and throat and then hungrily down upon her breast. But here he drew back.

"Naw," he said sternly to himself, "ah ain't goin' ter play her wid no loaded dice." Then quickly he covered her with the blanket to her chin, kissed her again upon the lips and tipped down into the darkness of the vestibule.

"Ah reckon ah bettah git married," he soliloquized. "B'lieve me, ah will, an' go uptown wid dicties."

He lit a cigar and stood there on the steps puffing and thinking for some time. His name was called inside the sitting room several times but he pretended not to hear. At last he stole back into the room where slept the girl who unwittingly and unwillingly was making him do queer things. He tipped up to the bed again and knelt there holding her hands so fiercely that she groaned without waking. He watched her and he wanted her so that he wished to crush her in his love; crush and crush and hurt her against himself, but somehow he resisted the impulse and merely kissed her lips again, kissed her hands back and front, removed the largest diamond ring from his hand and slipped it on her engagement finger. It was much too large so he closed her hand and tucked it securely beneath the covers.

"She's *mine*," he said triumphantly, "all mine!"

He switched off the light and softly closed the door as he went out again to the steps. He had gone up to the bedroom from the sitting room boldly, caring not who knew that Muttsy Owens took what he wanted. He was stealing forth afraid that someone might *suspect* that he had been there. There is no secret love in those barrens; it is a thing to be approached boisterously and without delay or dalliance. One loves when one wills, and ceases when it palls. There is nothing sacred or hidden — all subject to coarse jokes. So Muttsy re-entered the sitting room from the steps as if he had been into the street.

"Where you been Muttsy?" whined Ada with an awkward attempt at coyness.

"What *you* wanta know for?" he asked roughly.

"Now, Muttsy you know you ain't treatin' me right, honey. How come you runnin' de hawg ovah me lak you do?"

"Git outa mah face 'oman. Keep yo' han's offa me." He clapped on his hat and strode from the house.

Pinkie awoke with a gripping stomach and thumping head.

Ma bustled in. "How yuh feelin' darlin'? Youse jes' lak a li'l dol baby."

"I got a headache, terrible from that ole whiskey. Thass mah first und las' drink long as I live." She felt the ring.

"Whut's this?" she asked and drew her hand out to the light.

"Dat's Muttsy' ring. Ah seen him wid it fuh two years. How'd y'all make out? He sho is one thur'bred."

"Muttsy? When? I didn't see no Muttsy."

"Dearie, you doan' hafta tell yo' bizniss ef you doan wanta. Ahm a hush-mouf. Thass all right, keep yo' bizniss to yo' self." Ma bleared her eyes wisely. "But ah know Muttsy wuz up heah tuh see yuh las' night. Doan mine *me*, honey, gwan wid 'im. He'll treat yuh right. Ah *knows* he's crazy 'bout yuh. An' all de women is crazy 'bout *him*. Lawd! Lookit dat ring!" Ma regarded it greedily for a long time, but she turned and walked toward the door at last. "Git up darlin'. Ah got fried chicken fuh breakfus' un mush melon."

She went on to the kitchen. Ma's revelation sunk deeper, then there was the ring. Pinkie hurled the ring across the room and leaped out of bed.

"He ain't goin' to make *me* one of his women — I'll die first! I'm goin' outa this house if I starve, lemme starve!"

She got up and plunged her face into the cold water on the washstand in the corner and hurled herself into the shabby clothes, thrust the three dollars which she had never had occasion to spend under the pillow where Ma would be sure to find them and slipped noiselessly out of the house and fled down Fifth Avenue toward the park that marked the beginning of the Barrens. She did not know where she was going, and cared little so long as she removed herself as far as possible from the house where the great evil threatened her.

At ten o'clock that same morning, Muttsy Owens dressed his flashiest best, drove up to Ma's door in a cab, the most luxurious that could be hired. He had gone so far as to stick two one-hundred dollar notes to the inside of the windshield. Ma was overcome.

"Muttsy, dearie, what you doin' heah so soon? Pinkie sho has got you goin'. Un in a swell cab too — gee!"

"Ah'm gointer git mah'ried tuh de doll baby, thass how come. An' Ah'm gointer treat her white too."

"Umhumh! Thass how come de ring! You oughtn't never fuhgit me, Muttsy, fuh puttin' y'all together. But ah never thought you'd mah'ry *nobody* — you allus said you wouldn't."

"An ah wouldn't neither ef ah hadn't of seen *her*. Where she is?"

"In de room dressin'. She never tole me nothin' 'bout dis."

"She doan' know. She wuz 'sleep when ah made up mah mind an' slipped on de ring. But ah never miss no girl ah wants, you knows me."

"Everybody in this man's town knows you gets whut you wants."

"Naw, ah come tuh take her to break'fus 'fo we goes tuh de cotehouse."

"An' y'all stay heah and eat wid me. You go call her whilst ah set de grub on the table."

Muttsy, with a lordly stride, went up to Pinkie's door and rapped and waited and rapped and waited three times. Growing impatient or thinking her still asleep, he flung open the door and entered.

The first thing that struck him was the empty bed; the next was the glitter of his diamond ring upon the floor. He stumbled out to Ma. She was gone, no doubt of that.

"She looked awful funny when ah tole her you wuz in heah, but ah thought she wuz puttin' on airs," Ma declared finally.

"She thinks ah played wid a marked deck, but ah didn't. Ef ah could see her she'd love me. Ah know she would. 'Cause ah'd make her," Muttsy lamented.

"I don't know, Muttsy. She ain't no New Yorker, and she thinks gamblin' is awful."

"Zat all she got against me? Ah'll fix that up in a minute. You help me find her and ah'll do anything she says jus' so she marries me." He laughed ruefully. "Looks like ah crapped this time, don't it, Ma?"

The next day Muttsy was foreman of two hundred stevedores. How he did make them work. But oh how cheerfully they did their best for him. The company begrudged not one cent of his pay. He searched diligently, paid money to other searchers, went every night to Ma's to see if by chance the girl had returned or if any clues had turned up.

Two weeks passed this way. Black empty days for Muttsy.

Then he found her. He was coming home from work. When

crossing Seventh Avenue at 135th Street they almost collided. He seized her and began pleading before she even had time to recognize him.

He turned and followed her; took the employment office slip from her hand and destroyed it, took her arm and held it. He must have been very convincing for at 125th Street they entered a taxi that headed uptown again. Muttsy was smiling amiably upon the whole round world.

A month later, as Muttsy stood on the dock hustling his men to greater endeavor, Bluefront flashed past with his truck. "Say, Muttsy, you don't know what you missin' since you quit de game. Ah cleaned out de whole bunch las' night." He flashed a roll and laughed. "It don't seem like a month ago you wuz king uh de bones in Harlem." He vanished down the gangplank into the ship's hold.

As he raced back up the gangplank with his loaded truck Muttsy answered him. "And now, I'm king of the boneheads — stevedores. Come on over behind dis crate wid yo' roll. Mah wrist ain't got no cramp 'cause ah'm married. Youse gettin' too sassy."

"Thought you wuzn't gointer shoot no mo'!" Bluefront temporized.

"Aw Hell! Come on back heah," he said impatiently. "Ah'll shoot you any way you wants to — hard or soft roll — youse trying to stall. You know ah don't crap neither. Come on, mah Pinkie needs a fur coat and you stevedores is got to buy it."

He was on his knees with Bluefront. There was a quick movement of Muttsy's wrist, and the cubes flew out on a piece of burlap spread for the purpose — a perfect seven.

"Hot dog!" he exulted. "Look at dem babies gallop!" His wrist quivered again. "Nine for point!" he gloated. "Hah!" There was another quick shake and nine turned up again.

"Shove in, Bluefront, shove in dat roll, dese babies is crying fuh it."

Bluefront laid down two dollars grudgingly. "You said you wuzn't gointer roll no mo' dice after you got married," he grumbled.

But Muttsy had tasted blood. His flexible wrist was already in the midst of the next play.

"Come on, Bluefront, stop bellyachin'. Ah shoots huy for de roll!" He reached for his own pocket and laid down a roll of yellow bills beside Bluefront's. His hand quivered and the cubes skipped out again. "Nine!" He snapped his fingers like a trap-drum and gathered in the money.

"Doxology, Bluefront. Git back in de line wid yo' truck an' send de others roun' heah one by one. What man can't keep one li'l wife an' two li'l bones? Hurry 'em up, Blue!"

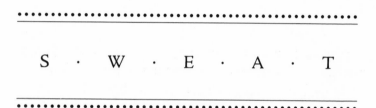

S · W · E · A · T

IT WAS ELEVEN o'clock of a Spring night in Florida. It was Sunday. Any other night, Delia Jones would have been in bed for two hours by this time. But she was a washwoman, and Monday morning meant a great deal to her. So she collected the soiled clothes on Saturday when she returned the clean things. Sunday night after church, she sorted and put the white things to soak. It saved her almost a half-day's start. A great hamper in the bedroom held the clothes that she brought home. It was so much neater than a number of bundles lying around.

She squatted on the kitchen floor beside the great pile of clothes, sorting them into small heaps according to color, and humming a song in a mournful key, but wondering through it all where Sykes, her husband, had gone with her horse and buckboard.

Just then something long, round, limp and black fell upon her shoulders and slithered to the floor beside her. A great terror took hold of her. It softened her knees and dried her mouth so that it was a full minute before she could cry out or move. Then she saw that it was the big bull whip her husband liked to carry when he drove.

She lifted her eyes to the door and saw him standing there bent over with laughter at her fright. She screamed at him.

"Sykes, what you throw dat whip on me like dat? You know it would skeer me — looks just like a snake, an' you knows how skeered Ah is of snakes."

"Course Ah knowed it! That's how come Ah done it." He slapped his leg with his hand and almost rolled on the ground in his mirth. "If you such a big fool dat you got to have a fit over a earth worm or a string, Ah don't keer how bad Ah skeer you."

"You ain't got no business doing it. Gawd knows it's a sin. Some day Ah'm gointuh drop dead from some of yo' foolishness. 'Nother thing, where you been wid mah rig? Ah feeds dat pony. He ain't fuh you to be drivin' wid no bull whip."

"You sho' is one aggravatin' nigger woman!" he declared and stepped into the room. She resumed her work and did not answer him at once. "Ah done tole you time and again to keep them white folks' clothes outa dis house."

He picked up the whip and glared at her. Delia went on with her work. She went out into the yard and returned with a galvanized tub and set it on the washbench. She saw that Sykes had kicked all of the clothes together again, and now stood in her way truculently, his whole manner hoping, *praying*, for an argument. But she walked calmly around him and commenced to re-sort the things.

"Next time, Ah'm gointer kick 'em outdoors," he threatened as he struck a match along the leg of his corduroy breeches.

Delia never looked up from her work, and her thin, stooped shoulders sagged further.

"Ah ain't for no fuss t'night Sykes. Ah just come from taking sacrament at the church house."

He snorted scornfully. "Yeah, you just come from de church

house on a Sunday night, but heah you is gone to work on them clothes. You ain't nothing but a hypocrite. One of them amen-corner Christians — sing, whoop, and shout, then come home and wash white folks' clothes on the Sabbath."

He stepped roughly upon the whitest pile of things, kicking them helter-skelter as he crossed the room. His wife gave a little scream of dismay, and quickly gathered them together again.

"Sykes, you quit grindin' dirt into these clothes! How can Ah git through by Sat'day if Ah don't start on Sunday?"

"Ah don't keer if you never git through. Anyhow, Ah done promised Gawd and a couple of other men, Ah ain't gointer have it in mah house. Don't gimme no lip neither, else Ah'll throw 'em out and put mah fist up side yo' head to boot."

Delia's habitual meekness seemed to slip from her shoulders like a blown scarf. She was on her feet; her poor little body, her bare knuckly hands bravely defying the strapping hulk before her.

"Looka heah, Sykes, you done gone too fur. Ah been married to you fur fifteen years, and Ah been takin' in washin' fur fifteen years. Sweat, sweat, sweat! Work and sweat, cry and sweat, pray and sweat!"

"What's that got to do with me?" he asked brutally.

"What's it got to do with you, Sykes? Mah tub of suds is filled yo' belly with vittles more times than yo' hands is filled it. Mah sweat is done paid for this house and Ah reckon Ah kin keep on sweatin' in it."

She seized the iron skillet from the stove and struck a defensive pose, which act surprised him greatly, coming from her. It cowed him and he did not strike her as he usually did.

"Naw you won't," she panted, "that ole snaggle-toothed black woman you runnin' with ain't comin' heah to pile up on *mah* sweat and blood. You ain't paid for nothin' on this place, and Ah'm gointer stay right heah till Ah'm toted out foot foremost."

"Well, you better quit gittin' me riled up, else they'll be totin' you out sooner than you expect. Ah'm so tired of you Ah don't know whut to do. Gawd! How Ah hates skinny wimmen!"

A little awed by this new Delia, he sidled out of the door and slammed the back gate after him. He did not say where he had gone, but she knew too well. She knew very well that he would not return until nearly daybreak also. Her work over, she went on to bed but not to sleep at once. Things had come to a pretty pass!

She lay awake, gazing upon the debris that cluttered their matrimonial trail. Not an image left standing along the way. Anything like flowers had long ago been drowned in the salty stream that had been pressed from her heart. Her tears, her sweat, her blood. She had brought love to the union and he had brought a longing after the flesh. Two months after the wedding, he had given her the first brutal beating. She had the memory of his numerous trips to Orlando with all of his wages when he had returned to her penniless, even before the first year had passed. She was young and soft then, but now she thought of her knotty, muscled limbs, her harsh knuckly hands, and drew herself up into an unhappy little ball in the middle of the big feather bed. Too late now to hope for love, even if it were not Bertha it would be someone else. This case differed from the others only in that she was bolder than the others. Too late for everything except her little home. She had built it for her old days, and planted one by one the trees and flowers there. It was lovely to her, lovely.

Somehow, before sleep came, she found herself saying aloud: "Oh well, whatever goes over the Devil's back, is got to come under his belly. Sometime or ruther, Sykes, like everybody else, is gointer reap his sowing." After that she was able to build a spiritual earthworks against her husband. His shells could no longer reach her. AMEN. She went to sleep and slept until he announced his presence in bed by kicking her feet and rudely snatching the covers away.

"Gimme some kivah heah, an' git yo' damn foots over on yo' own side! Ah oughter mash you in yo' mouf fuh drawing dat skillet on me."

Delia went clear to the rail without answering him. A triumphant indifference to all that he was or did.

II

The week was as full of work for Delia as all other weeks, and Saturday found her behind her little pony, collecting and delivering clothes.

It was a hot, hot day near the end of July. The village men on Joe Clarke's porch even chewed cane listlessly. They did not hurl the cane-knots as usual. They let them dribble over the edge of the porch. Even conversation had collapsed under the heat.

"Heah come Delia Jones," Jim Merchant said, as the shaggy pony came 'round the bend of the road toward them. The rusty buckboard was heaped with baskets of crisp, clean laundry.

"Yep," Joe Lindsay agreed. "Hot or col', rain or shine, jes'ez reg'lar ez de weeks roll roun' Delia carries 'em an' fetches 'em on Sat'day."

"She better if she wanter eat," said Moss. "Syke Jones ain't wuth de shot an' powder hit would tek tuh kill 'em. Not to *huh* he ain't."

"He sho' ain't," Walter Thomas chimed in. "It's too bad,

too, cause she wuz a right pretty li'l trick when he got huh.
Ah'd uh mah'ied huh mahself if he hadnter beat me to it."

Delia nodded briefly at the men as she drove past.

"Too much knockin' will ruin *any* 'oman. He done beat huh
'nough tuh kill three women, let 'lone change they looks," said
Elijah Moseley. "How Syke kin stommuck dat big black greasy
Mogul he's layin' roun' wid, gits me. Ah swear dat eight-rock
couldn't kiss a sardine can Ah done thowed out de back do'
'way las' yeah."

"Aw, she's fat, thass how come. He's allus been crazy 'bout
fat women," put in Merchant. "He'd a' been tied up wid one
long time ago if he could a' found one tuh have him. Did Ah
tell yuh 'bout him come sidlin' roun' *mah* wife — bringin' her a
basket uh peecans outa his yard fuh a present? Yessir, mah
wife! She tol' him tuh take 'em right straight back home, 'cause
Delia works so hard ovah dat washtub she reckon everything
on de place taste lak sweat an' soapsuds. Ah jus' wisht Ah'd a'
caught 'im 'roun' dere! Ah'd a' made his hips ketch on fiah
down dat shell road."

"Ah know he done it, too. Ah sees 'im grinnin' at every
'oman dat passes," Walter Thomas said. "But even so, he useter
eat some mighty big hunks uh humble pie tuh git dat li'l 'oman
he got. She wuz ez pritty ez a speckled pup! Dat wuz fifteen
years ago. He useter be so skeered uh losin' huh, she could
make him do some parts of a husband's duty. Dey never wuz de
same in de mind."

"There oughter be a law about him," said Lindsay. "He ain't
fit tuh carry guts tuh a bear."

Clarke spoke for the first time. "Tain't no law on earth dat
kin make a man be decent if it ain't in 'im. There's plenty men
dat takes a wife lak dey do a joint uh sugar-cane. It's round,
juicy an' sweet when dey gits it. But dey squeeze an' grind,

squeeze an' grind an' wring tell dey wring every drop uh pleasure dat's in 'em out. When dey's satisfied dat dey is wrung dry, dey treats 'em jes' lak dey do a cane-chew. Dey thows 'em away. Dey knows whut dey is doin' while dey is at it, an' hates theirselves fuh it but they keeps on hangin' after huh tell she's empty. Den dey hates huh fuh bein' a cane-chew an' in de way."

"We oughter take Syke an' dat stray 'oman uh his'n down in Lake Howell swamp an' lay on de rawhide till they cain't say Lawd a' mussy. He allus wuz uh ovahbearin niggah, but since dat white 'oman from up north done teached 'im how to run a automobile, he done got too beggety to live — an' we oughter kill 'im," Old Man Anderson advised.

A grunt of approval went around the porch. But the heat was melting their civic virtue and Elijah Moseley began to bait Joe Clarke.

"Come on, Joe, git a melon outa dere an' slice it up for yo' customers. We'se all sufferin' wid de heat. De bear's done got me!"

"Thass right, Joe, a watermelon is jes' whut Ah needs tuh cure de eppizudicks," Walter Thomas joined forces with Moseley. "Come on dere, Joe. We all is steady customers an' you ain't set us up in a long time. Ah chooses dat long, bowlegged Floridy favorite."

"A god, an' be dough. You all gimme twenty cents and slice away," Clarke retorted. "Ah needs a col' slice m'self. Heah, everybody chip in. Ah'll lend y'all mah meat knife."

The money was all quickly subscribed and the huge melon brought forth. At that moment, Sykes and Bertha arrived. A determined silence fell on the porch and the melon was put away again.

Merchant snapped down the blade of his jackknife and moved toward the store door.

"Come on in, Joe, an' gimme a slab uh sow belly an' uh pound uh coffee — almost fuhgot 'twas Sat'day. Got to git on home." Most of the men left also.

Just then Delia drove past on her way home, as Sykes was ordering magnificently for Bertha. It pleased him for Delia to see.

"Git whutsoever yo' heart desires, Honey. Wait a minute, Joe. Give huh two bottles uh strawberry soda-water, uh quart parched ground-peas, an' a block uh chewin' gum."

With all this they left the store, with Sykes reminding Bertha that this was his town and she could have it if she wanted it.

The men returned soon after they left, and held their watermelon feast.

"Where did Syke Jones git da 'oman from nohow?" Lindsay asked.

"Ovah Apopka. Guess dey musta been cleanin' out de town when she lef'. She don't look lak a thing but a hunk uh liver wid hair on it."

"Well, she sho' kin squall," Dave Carter contributed. "When she gits ready tuh laff, she jes' opens huh mouf an' latches it back tuh de las' notch. No ole granpa alligator down in Lake Bell ain't got nothin' on huh."

III

Bertha had been in town three months now. Sykes was still paying her room-rent at Della Lewis' — the only house in town that would have taken her in. Sykes took her frequently to Winter Park to 'stomps'. He still assured her that he was the swellest man in the state.

"Sho' you kin have dat li'l ole house soon's Ah git dat 'oman outa dere. Everything b'longs tuh me an' you sho' kin have it.

Ah sho' 'bominates uh skinny 'oman. Lawdy, you sho' is got one portly shape on you! You kin git *anything* you wants. Dis is *mah* town an' you sho' kin have it."

Delia's work-worn knees crawled over the earth in Gethsemane and up the rocks of Calvary many, many times during these months. She avoided the villagers and meeting places in her efforts to be blind and deaf. But Bertha nullified this to a degree, by coming to Delia's house to call Sykes out to her at the gate.

Delia and Sykes fought all the time now with no peaceful interludes. They slept and ate in silence. Two or three times Delia had attempted a timid friendliness, but she was repulsed each time. It was plain that the breaches must remain agape.

The sun had burned July to August. The heat streamed down like a million hot arrows, smiting all things living upon the earth. Grass withered, leaves browned, snakes went blind in shedding and men and dogs went mad. Dog days!

Delia came home one day and found Sykes there before her. She wondered, but started to go on into the house without speaking, even though he was standing in the kitchen door and she must either stoop under his arm or ask him to move. He made no room for her. She noticed a soap box beside the steps, but paid no particular attention to it, knowing that he must have brought it there. As she was stooping to pass under his outstretched arm, he suddenly pushed her backward, laughingly.

"Look in de box dere Delia, Ah done brung yuh somethin'!"

She nearly fell upon the box in her stumbling, and when she saw what it held, she all but fainted outright.

"Syke! Syke, mah Gawd! You take dat rattlesnake 'way from heah! You *gottuh*. Oh, Jesus, have mussy!"

"Ah ain't got tuh do nuthin' uh de kin'—fact is Ah ain't got tuh do nothin' but die. Tain't no use uh you puttin' on airs makin' out lak you skeered uh dat snake—he's gointer stay right heah tell he die. He wouldn't bite me cause Ah knows how tuh handle 'im. Nohow he wouldn't risk breakin' out his fangs 'gin *yo* skinny laigs."

"Naw, now Syke, don't keep dat thing 'round tryin' tuh skeer me tuh death. You knows Ah'm even feared uh earth worms. Thass de biggest snake Ah evah did see. Kill 'im Syke, please."

"Doan ast me tuh do nothin' fuh yuh. Goin' 'round tryin' tuh be so damn asterperious. Naw, Ah ain't gonna kill it. Ah think uh damn sight mo' uh him dan you! Dat's a nice snake an' anybody doan lak 'im kin jes' hit de grit."

The village soon heard that Sykes had the snake, and came to see and ask questions.

"How de hen-fire did you ketch dat six-foot rattler, Syke?" Thomas asked.

"He's full uh frogs so he cain't hardly move, thass how Ah eased up on 'm. But Ah'm a snake charmer an' knows how tuh handle 'em. Shux, dat ain't nothin'. Ah could ketch one eve'y day if Ah so wanted tuh."

"Whut he needs is a heavy hick'ry club leaned real heavy on his head. Dat's de bes' way tuh charm a rattlesnake."

"Naw, Walt, y'all jes' don't understand dese diamon' backs lak Ah do," said Sykes in a superior tone of voice.

The village agreed with Walter, but the snake stayed on. His box remained by the kitchen door with its screen wire covering. Two or three days later it had digested its meal of frogs and literally came to life. It rattled at every movement in the kitchen or the yard. One day as Delia came down the kitchen steps she saw his chalky-white fangs curved like scimitars hung in the wire meshes. This time she did not run away with averted eyes as usual. She stood for a long time in the

doorway in a red fury that grew bloodier for every second that
she regarded the creature that was her torment.

That night she broached the subject as soon as Sykes sat
down to the table.

"Syke, Ah wants you tuh take dat snake 'way fum heah. You
done starved me an' Ah put up widcher, you done beat me an
Ah took dat, but you done kilt all mah insides bringin' dat
varmint heah."

Sykes poured out a saucer full of coffee and drank it
deliberately before he answered her.

"A whole lot Ah keer 'bout how you feels inside uh out. Dat
snake ain't goin' no damn wheah till Ah gits ready fuh 'im tuh
go. So fur as beatin' is concerned, yuh ain't took near all dat
you gointer take ef yuh stay 'round *me*."

Delia pushed back her plate and got up from the table. "Ah
hates you, Sykes," she said calmly. "Ah hates you tuh de same
degree dat Ah useter love yuh. Ah done took an' took till mah
belly is full up tuh mah neck. Dat's de reason Ah got mah letter
fum de church an' moved mah membership tuh Woodbridge —
so Ah don't haftuh take no sacrament wid yuh. Ah don't wantuh
see yuh 'round me atall. Lay 'round wid dat 'oman all yuh wants
tuh, but gwan 'way fum me an' mah house. Ah hates yuh lak uh
suck-egg dog."

Sykes almost let the huge wad of corn bread and collard
greens he was chewing fall out of his mouth in amazement. He
had a hard time whipping himself up to the proper fury to try
to answer Delia.

"Well, Ah'm glad you does hate me. Ah'm sho' tiahed uh
you hangin' ontuh me. Ah don't want yuh. Look at yuh stringey
ole neck! Yo' rawbony laigs an' arms is enough tuh cut uh man
tuh death. You looks jes' lak de devvul's doll-baby tuh *me*. You

cain't hate me no worse dan Ah hates you. Ah been hatin' *you* fuh years."

"Yo' ole black hide don't look lak nothin' tuh me, but uh passle uh wrinkled up rubber, wid yo' big ole yeahs flappin' on each side lak uh paih uh buzzard wings. Don't think Ah'm gointuh be run 'way fum mah house neither. Ah'm goin' tuh de white folks 'bout *you*, mah young man, de very nex' time you lay yo' han's on me. Mah cup is done run ovah." Delia said this with no signs of fear and Sykes departed from the house, threatening her, but made not the slightest move to carry out any of them.

That night he did not return at all, and the next day being Sunday, Delia was glad she did not have to quarrel before she hitched up her pony and drove the four miles to Woodbridge.

She stayed to the night service — 'love feast' — which was very warm and full of spirit. In the emotional winds her domestic trials were borne far and wide so that she sang as she drove homeward,

> *Jurden water, black an' col*
> *Chills de body, not de soul*
> *An' Ah wantah cross Jurden in uh calm time.*

She came from the barn to the kitchen door and stopped.

"Whut's de mattah, ol' Satan, you ain't kickin' up yo' racket?" She addressed the snake's box. Complete silence. She went on into the house with a new hope in its birth struggles. Perhaps her threat to go to the white folks had frightened Sykes! Perhaps he was sorry! Fifteen years of misery and suppression had brought Delia to the place where she would hope *anything* that looked towards a way over or through her wall of inhibitions.

She felt in the match-safe behind the stove at once for a match. There was only one there.

"Dat niggah wouldn't fetch nothin' heah tuh save his rotten neck, but he kin run thew whut Ah brings quick enough. Now he done toted off nigh on tuh haff uh box uh matches. He done had dat 'oman heah in mah house, too."

Nobody but a woman could tell how she knew this even before she struck the match. But she did and it put her into a new fury.

Presently she brought in the tubs to put the white things to soak. This time she decided she need not bring the hamper out of the bedroom; she would go in there and do the sorting. She picked up the pot-bellied lamp and went in. The room was small and the hamper stood hard by the foot of the white iron bed. She could sit and reach through the bedposts — resting as she worked.

"*Ah wantah cross Jurden in uh calm time.*" She was singing again. The mood of the 'love feast' had returned. She threw back the lid of the basket almost gaily. Then, moved by both horror and terror, she sprang back toward the door. *There lay the snake in the basket!* He moved sluggishly at first, but even as she turned round and round, jumped up and down in an insanity of fear, he began to stir vigorously. She saw him pouring his awful beauty from the basket upon the bed, then she seized the lamp and ran as fast as she could to the kitchen. The wind from the open door blew out the light and the darkness added to her terror. She sped to the darkness of the yard, slamming the door after her before she thought to set down the lamp. She did not feel safe even on the ground, so she climbed up in the hay barn.

There for an hour or more she lay sprawled upon the hay a gibbering wreck.

Finally she grew quiet, and after that came coherent thought.

With this stalked through her a cold, bloody rage. Hours of this. A period of introspection, a space of retrospection, then a mixture of both. Out of this an awful calm.

"Well, Ah done de bes' Ah could. If things ain't right, Gawd knows tain't mah fault."

She went to sleep — a twitch sleep — and woke up to a faint gray sky. There was a loud hollow sound below. She peered out. Sykes was at the wood-pile, demolishing a wire-covered box.

He hurried to the kitchen door, but hung outside there some minutes before he entered, and stood some minutes more inside before he closed it after him.

The gray in the sky was spreading. Delia descended without fear now, and crouched beneath the low bedroom window. The drawn shade shut out the dawn, shut in the night. But the thin walls held back no sound.

"Dat ol' scratch is woke up now!" She mused at the tremendous whirr inside, which every woodsman knows, is one of the sound illusions. The rattler is a ventriloquist. His whirr sounds to the right, to the left, straight ahead, behind, close under foot — everywhere but where it is. Woe to him who guesses wrong unless he is prepared to hold up his end of the argument! Sometimes he strikes without rattling at all.

Inside, Sykes heard nothing until he knocked a pot lid off the stove while trying to reach the match-safe in the dark. He had emptied his pockets at Bertha's.

The snake seemed to wake up under the stove and Sykes made a quick leap into the bedroom. In spite of the gin he had had, his head was clearing now.

"Mah Gawd!" he chattered, "ef Ah could on'y strack uh light!"

The rattling ceased for a moment as he stood paralyzed. He

waited. It seemed that the snake waited also.

"Oh, fuh de light! Ah thought he'd be too sick" — Sykes was muttering to himself when the whirr began again, closer, right underfoot this time. Long before this, Sykes' ability to think had been flattened down to primitive instinct and he leaped — onto the bed.

Outside Delia heard a cry that might have come from a maddened chimpanzee, a stricken gorilla. All the terror, all the horror, all the rage that man possibly could express, without a recognizable human sound.

A tremendous stir inside there, another series of animal screams, the intermittent whirr of the reptile. The shade torn violently down from the window, letting in the red dawn, a huge brown hand seizing the window stick, great dull blows upon the wooden floor punctuating the gibberish of sound long after the rattle of the snake had abruptly subsided. All this Delia could see and hear from her place beneath the window, and it made her ill. She crept over to the four-o'clocks and stretched herself on the cool earth to recover.

She lay there. "Delia, Delia!" She could hear Sykes calling in a most despairing tone as one who expected no answer. The sun crept on up, and he called. Delia could not move — her legs had gone flabby. She never moved, he called, and the sun kept rising.

"Mah Gawd!" She heard him moan, "Mah Gawd fum Heben!" She heard him stumbling about and got up from her flower-bed. The sun was growing warm. As she approached the door she heard him call out hopefully, "Delia, is dat you Ah heah?"

She saw him on his hands and knees as soon as she reached the door. He crept an inch or two toward her — all that he was able, and she saw his horribly swollen neck and his one open eye shining with hope. A surge of pity too strong to support bore her away from that eye that must, could not, fail to see the tubs. He would see the lamp. Orlando with its doctors was too far. She could scarcely reach the chinaberry tree, where she waited in the growing heat while inside she knew the cold river was creeping up and up to extinguish that eye which must know by now that she knew.

T·H·E G·I·L·D·E·D
S·I·X·B·I·T·S

IT WAS A Negro yard around a Negro house in a Negro settlement that looked to the payroll of the G and G Fertilizer works for its support.

But there was something happy about the place. The front yard was parted in the middle by a sidewalk from gate to doorstep, a sidewalk edged on either side by quart bottles driven neck down to the ground on a slant. A mess of homey flowers planted without a plan but blooming cheerily from their helter-skelter places. The fence and house were whitewashed. The porch and steps scrubbed white.

The front door stood open to the sunshine so that the floor of the front room could finish drying after its weekly scouring. It was Saturday. Everything clean from the front gate to the privy house. Yard raked so that the strokes of the rake would make a pattern. Fresh newspaper cut in fancy-edge on the kitchen shelves.

Missie May was bathing herself in the galvanized washtub in the bedroom. Her dark-brown skin glistened under the soapsuds that skittered down from her wash rag. Her stiff young breasts thrust forward aggressively like broad-based cones with the tips lacquered in black.

She heard men's voices in the distance and glanced at the dollar clock on the dresser.

"Humph! Ah'm way behind time t'day! Joe gointer be heah 'fore Ah git mah clothes on if Ah don't make haste."

She grabbed the clean meal sack at hand and dried herself hurriedly and began to dress. But before she could tie her slippers, there came the ring of singing metal on wood. Nine times.

Missie May grinned with delight. She had not seen the big tall man come stealing in the gate and creep up the walk grinning happily at the joyful mischief he was about to commit. But she knew that it was her husband throwing silver dollars in the door for her to pick up and pile beside her plate at dinner. It was this way every Saturday afternoon. The nine dollars hurled into the open door, he scurried to a hiding place behind the cape jasmine bush and waited.

Missie May promptly appeared at the door in mock alarm.

"Who dat chunkin' money in mah do'way?" she demanded. No answer from the yard. She leaped off the porch and began to search the shrubbery. She peeped under the porch and hung over the gate to look up and down the road. While she did this, the man behind the jasmine darted to the chinaberry tree. She spied him and gave chase.

"Nobody ain't gointer be chunkin' money at me and Ah not do'em nothin'," she shouted in mock anger. He ran around the house with Missie May at his heels. She overtook him at the kitchen door. He ran inside but could not close it after him before she crowded in and locked with him in a rough and tumble. For several minutes the two were a furious mass of male and female energy. Shouting, laughing, twisting, turning, and Joe trying, but not too hard, to get away.

"Missie May, take yo' hand out mah pocket!" Joe shouted out between laughs.

"Ah ain't, Joe, not lessen you gwine gimme whateve' it is good you got in yo' pocket. Turn it go Joe, do Ah'll tear yo' clothes."

"Go on tear 'em. You de one dat pushes de needles round heah. Move yo' hand Missie May."

"Lemme git dat paper sack out yo' pocket. Ah bet its candy kisses."

"Tain't. Move yo' hand. Woman ain't got no business in a man's clothes nohow. Go 'way."

Missie May gouged way down and gave an upward jerk and triumphed.

"Unhhunh! Ah got it. It 'tis so candy kisses. Ah knowed you had somethin' for me in yo' clothes. Now Ah got to see whut's in every pocket you got."

Joe smiled indulgently and let his wife go through all of his pockets and take out the things that he had hidden there for her to find. She bore off the chewing gum, the cake of sweet soap, the pocket handkerchief as if she had wrested them from him, as if they had not been bought for the sake of this friendly battle.

"Whew! dat play-fight done got me all warmed up," Joe exclaimed. "Got me some water in de kittle?"

"Yo' water is on de fire and yo' clean things is cross de bed. Hurry up and wash yo'self and git changed so we kin eat. Ah'm hongry." As Missie said this, she bore the steaming kettle into the bedroom.

"You ain't hongry, sugar," Joe contradicted her. "Youse jes's little empty. Ah'm de one whut's hongry. Ah could eat up camp meetin,' back off 'ssociation, and drink Jurdan dry. Have it on de table when Ah git out de tub."

"Don't you mess wid mah business, man. You git in yo' clothes. Ah'm a real wife, not no dress and breath. Ah might not look lak one, but if you burn me, you won't git a thing but wife ashes."

Joe splashed in the bedroom and Missie May fanned around in the kitchen. A fresh red and white checked cloth on the table. Big pitcher of buttermilk beaded with pale drops of butter from the churn. Hot fried mullet, crackling bread, ham hocks atop a mound of string beans and new potatoes, and perched on the window-sill a pone of spicy potato pudding.

Very little talk during the meal but that little consisted of banter that pretended to deny affection but in reality flaunted it. Like when Missie May reached for a second helping of the tater pone. Joe snatched it out of her reach. After Missie May had made two or three unsuccessful grabs at the pan, she begged, "Aw, Joe gimme some mo' dat tater pone."

"Nope, sweetenin' is for us men-folks. Y'all pritty li'l frail eels don't need nothin' lak dis. You too sweet already."

"Please, Joe."

"Naw, naw. Ah don't want you to git no sweeter than whut you is already. We goin' down de road al li'l piece t'night so you go put on yo' Sunday-go-to-meetin' things."

Missie May looked at her husband to see if he was playing some prank. "Sho' nuff, Joe?"

"Yeah. We goin' to de ice cream parlor."

"Where de ice cream parlor at, Joe?"

"A new man done come heah from Chicago and he done got a place and took and opened it up for a ice cream parlor, and bein' as it's real swell, Ah wants you to be one de first ladies to walk in dere and have some set down."

"Do Jesus, Ah ain't knowed nothin' 'bout it. Who de man done it?"

"Mister Otis D. Slemmons, of spots and places — Memphis, Chicago, Jacksonville, Philadelphia and so on."

"Dat heavy-set man wid his mouth full of gold teethes?"

"Yeah. Where did you see 'im at?"

"Ah went down to de sto' tuh git a box of lye and Ah seen 'im standin' on de corner talkin' to some of de mens, and Ah come on back and went to scrubbin' de floor, and he passed and tipped his hat whilst Ah was scourin' de steps. Ah thought never Ah seen *him* befo'."

Joe smiled pleasantly. "Yeah, he's up to date. He got de finest clothes Ah ever seen on a colored man's back."

"Aw, he don't look no better in his clothes than you do in yourn. He got a puzzlegut on 'im and he so chuckle-headed, he got a pone behind his neck."

Joe looked down at his own abdomen and said wistfully, "Wisht Ah had a build on me lak he got. He ain't puzzle-gutted, honey. He jes' got a corperation. Dat make 'm look lak a rich white man. All rich mens is got some belly on 'em."

"Ah seen de pitchers of Henry Ford and he's a spare-built man and Rockefeller look lak he ain't got but one gut. But Ford and Rockefeller and dis Slemmons and all de rest kin be as many-gutted as dey please, ah'm satisfied wid you jes' lak you is, baby. God took pattern after a pine tree and built you noble. Youse a pritty still man, and if Ah knowed any way to make you mo' pritty still Ah'd take and do it."

Joe reached over gently and toyed with Missie May's ear. "You jes' say dat cause you love me, but Ah know Ah can't hold no light to Otis D. Slemmons. Ah ain't never been nowhere and Ah ain't got nothin' but you."

"How you know dat, Joe."

"He tole us so hisself."

"Dat don't make it so. His mouf is cut cross-ways, ain't it? Well, he kin lie jes' lak anybody els."

"Good Lawd, Missie! You womens sho' is hard to sense into things. He's got a five-dollar gold piece for a stick-pin and he got a ten-dollar gold piece on his watch chain and his mouf is jes' crammed full of gold teethes. Sho' wisht it wuz mine. And whut make it so cool, he got money 'cumulated. And womens give it all to 'im."

"Ah don't see whut de womens see on 'im. Ah wouldn't give 'im a wind if de sherff wuz after 'im."

"Well, he tole us how de white womens in Chicago give 'im all dat gold money. So he don't 'low nobody to touch it at all. Not even put dey finger on it. Dey tole 'im not to. You kin make 'miration at it, but don't tetch it."

"Whyn't he stay up dere where dey so crazy 'bout 'im?"

"Ah reckon dey done made 'im vast-rich and he wants to travel some. He say dey wouldn't leave 'im hit a lick of work. He got mo' lady people crazy 'bout him than he kin shake a stick at."

"Joe, Ah hates to see you so dumb. Dat stray nigger jes' tell y'all anything and y'all b'lieve it."

"Go 'head on now, honey and put on yo' clothes. He talkin' 'bout his pritty womens—Ah want 'im to see *mine*."

Missie May went off to dress and Joe spent the time trying to make his stomach punch out like Slemmons' middle. He tried the rolling swagger of the stranger, but found that his tall bone-and-muscle stride fitted ill with it. He just had time to drop back into his seat before Missie May came in dressed to go.

On the way home that night Joe was exultant. "Didn't Ah say ole Otis was swell? Can't he talk Chicago talk? Wuzn't dat

funny whut he said when great big fat ole Ida Armstrong come
in? He asted me, " 'Who is dat broad wid de forty shake?'
Dat's a new word. Us always thought forty was a set of figgers
but he showed us where it means a whole heap of things.
Sometimes he don't say forty, he jes' say thirty-eight and two
and dat mean de same thing. Know whut he tole me when Ah
was payin' for our ice cream? He say, 'Ah have to hand it to
you, Joe. Dat wife of yours is jes' thirty-eight and two. Yessuh,
she's forty!' Ain't he killin'?"

"He'll do in case of a rush. But he sho' is got uh heap uh
gold on 'im. Dat's de first time Ah ever seed gold money. It
lookted good on him sho' nuff, but it'd look a whole heap better
on you."

"Who, me? Missie May was youse crazy! Where would a
po' man lak me git gold money from?"

Missie May was silent for a minute, then she said, "Us
might find some goin' long de road some time. Us could."

"Who would be losin' gold money 'round heah? We ain't
even seen none dese white folks wearin' no gold money on dey
watch chain. You must be figgeren' Mister Packard or Mister
Cadillac goin' pass through heah . . ."

"You don't know whut been lost 'round heah. Maybe somebody way back in memorial times lost they gold money and
went on off and it ain't never been found. And then if we wuz
to find it, you could wear some 'thout havin' no gang of womens
lak dat Slemmons say he got."

Joe laughed and hugged her. "Don't be so wishful 'bout me.
Ah'm satisfied de way Ah is. So long as Ah be yo' husband, ah
don't keer 'bout nothin' else. Ah'd ruther all de other womens
in de world to be dead than for you to have de toothache. Less
we go to bed and git our night rest."

It was Saturday night once more before Joe could parade

his wife in Slemmons' ice cream parlor again. He worked the night shift and Saturday was his only night off. Every other evening around six o'clock he left home, and dying dawn saw him hustling home around the lake where the challenging sun flung a flaming sword from east to west across the trembling water.

That was the best part of life — going home to Missie May. Their whitewashed house, the mock battle on Saturday, the dinner and ice cream parlor afterwards, church on Sunday nights when Missie outdressed any woman in town — all, everything was right.

One night around eleven the acid ran out at the G and G. The foreman knocked off the crew and let the steam die down. As Joe rounded the lake on his way home, a lean moon rode the lake in a silver boat. If anybody had asked Joe about the moon on the lake, he would have said he hadn't paid it any attention. But he saw it with his feelings. It made him yearn painfully for Missie. Creation obsessed him. He thought about children. They had been married for more than a year now. They had money put away. They ought to be making little feet for shoes. A little boy child would be about right.

He saw a dim light in the bedroom and decided to come in through the kitchen door. He could wash the fertilizer dust off himself before presenting himself to Missie May. It would be nice for her not to know that he was there until he slipped into his place in bed and hugged her back. She always liked that.

He eased the kitchen door open slowly and silently, but when he went to set his dinner bucket on the table he bumped it into a pile of dishes, and something crashed to the floor. He heard his wife gasp in fright and hurried to reassure her.

"Iss me, honey. Don't get skeered."

There was a quick, large movement in the bedroom. A

rustle, a thud, and a stealthy silence. The light went out.

What? Robbers? Murderers? Some varmint attacking his helpless wife, perhaps. He struck a match, threw himself on guard and stepped over the door-sill into the bedroom.

The great belt on the wheel of Time slipped and eternity stood still. By the match light he could see the man's legs fighting with his breeches in his frantic desire to get them on. He had both chance and time to kill the intruder in his helpless condition — half-in and half-out of his pants — but he was too weak to take action. The shapeless enemies of humanity that live in the hours of Time had waylaid Joe. He was assaulted in his weakness. Like Samson awakening after his haircut. So he just opened his mouth and laughed.

The match went out and he struck another and lit the lamp. A howling wind raced across his heart, but underneath its fury he heard his wife sobbing and Slemmons pleading for his life. Offering to buy it with all that he had. "Please, suh, don't kill me. Sixty-two dollars at de sto' gold money."

Joe just stood. Slemmons looked at the window, but it was screened. Joe stood out like a rough-backed mountain between him and the door. Barring him from escape, from sunrise, from life.

He considered a surprise attack upon the big clown that stood there laughing like a chessy cat. But before his fist could travel an inch, Joe's own rushed out to crush him like a battering ram. Then Joe stood over him.

"Git into yo' damn rags, Slemmons, and dat quick."

Slemmons scrambled to his feet and into his vest and coat. As he grabbed his hat, Joe's fury overrode his intentions and he grabbed at Slemmons with his left hand and struck at him with his right. The right landed. The left grazed the front of his vest. Slemmons was knocked a somersault into the kitchen and fled through the open door. Joe found himself alone with Missie May, with the golden watch charm clutched in his left fist. A short bit of broken chain dangled between his fingers.

Missie May was sobbing. Wails of weeping without words. Joe stood, and after awhile she found out that he had something in his hand. And then he stood and felt without thinking and without seeing with his natural eyes. Missie May kept on crying and Joe kept on feeling so much and not knowing what to do with all his feelings, he put Slemmons' watch charm in his pants pocket and took a good laugh and went to bed.

"Missie May, whut you crying for?"

"Cause Ah love you so hard and Ah know you don't love *me* no mo'."

Joe sank his face into the pillow for a spell then he said huskily, "You don't know de feelings of dat yet, Missie May."

"Oh Joe, honey, he said he wuz gointer gimme dat gold money and he jes' kept on after me — "

Joe was very still and silent for a long time. Then he said, "Well, don't cry no mo', Missie May. Ah got yo' gold piece for you."

The hours went past on their rusty ankles. Joe still and quiet on one bed-rail and Missie May wrung dry of sobs on the other. Finally the sun's tide crept upon the shore of night and drowned all its hours. Missie May with her face stiff and streaked towards the window saw the dawn come into her yard. It was day. Nothing more. Joe wouldn't be coming home as usual. No need to fling open the front door and sweep off the porch, making it nice for Joe. Never no more breakfast to cook; no more washing and starching of Joe's jumper-jackets and pants. No more nothing. So why get up?

With this strange man in her bed, she felt embarrassed to get up and dress. She decided to wait till he had dressed and gone. Then she would get up, dress quickly and be gone forever beyond reach of Joe's looks and laughs. But he never moved. Red light turned to yellow, then white.

From beyond the no-man's land between them came a voice. A strange voice that yesterday had been Joe's.

"Missie May, ain't you gonna fix me no breakfus'?"

She sprang out of bed. "Yeah, Joe. Ah didn't reckon you wuz hongry."

No need to die today. Joe needed her for a few more minutes anyhow.

Soon there was a roaring fire in the cook stove. Water bucket full and two chickens killed. Joe loved fried chicken and rice. She didn't deserve a thing and good Joe was letting her cook him some breakfast. She rushed hot biscuits to the table as Joe took his seat.

He ate with his eyes on his plate. No laughter, no banter.

"Missie May, you ain't eatin' yo' breakfus'."

"Ah don't choose none, Ah thank yuh."

His coffee cup was empty. She sprang to refill it. When she turned from the stove and bent to set the cup beside Joe's plate, she saw the yellow coin on the table between them.

She slumped into her seat and wept into her arms.

Presently Joe said calmly, "Missie May, you cry too much. Don't look back lak Lot's wife and turn to salt."

The sun, the hero of every day, the impersonal old man that beams as brightly on death as on birth, came up every morning and raced across the blue dome and dipped into the sea of fire every evening. Water ran down hill and birds nested.

Missie knew why she didn't leave Joe. She couldn't. She loved him too much. But she couldn't understand why Joe didn't leave her. He was polite, even kind at times, but aloof.

There were no more Saturday romps. No ringing silver dollars to stack beside her plate. No pockets to rifle. In fact the yellow coin in his trousers was like a monster hiding in the cave of his pockets to destroy her.

She often wondered if he still had it, but nothing could have induced her to ask nor yet to explore his pockets to see for herself. Its shadow was in the house whether or no.

One night Joe came home around midnight and complained of pains in the back. He asked Missie to rub him down with liniment. It had been three months since Missie had touched his body and it all seemed strange. But she rubbed him. Grateful for the chance. Before morning, youth triumphed and Missie exulted. But the next day, as she joyfully made up their bed, beneath her pillow she found the piece of money with the bit of chain attached.

Alone to herself, she looked at the thing with loathing, but look she must. She took it into her hands with trembling and saw first thing that it was no gold piece. It was a gilded half-dollar. Then she knew why Slemmons had forbidden anyone to touch his gold. He trusted village eyes at a distance not to recognize his stick-pin as a gilded quarter, and his watch charm as a four-bit piece.

She was glad at first that Joe had left it there. Perhaps he was through with her punishment. They were man and wife again. Then another thought came clawing at her. He had come home to buy from her as if she were any woman in the long house. Fifty cents for her love. As if to say that he could pay as well as Slemmons. She slid the coin into his Sunday pants pocket and dressed herself and left his house.

Halfway between her house and the quarters she met her husband's mother, and after a short talk she turned and went back home. If she had not the substance of marriage, she had the outside show. Joe must leave *her*. She let him see she didn't want his old gold four-bits too.

She saw no more of the coin for some time though she knew that Joe could not help finding it in his pocket. But his health kept poor, and he came home at least every ten days to be rubbed.

The sun swept around the horizon, trailing its robes of weeks and days. One morning as Joe came in from work, he found Missie May chopping wood. Without a word he took the ax and chopped a huge pile before he stopped.

"You ain't got no business choppin' wood, and you know it."

"How come? Ah been choppin' it for de last longest."

"Ah ain't blind. You makin' feet for shoes."

"Won't you be glad to have a li'l baby chile, Joe?"

"You know dat 'thout astin' me."

"Iss gointer be a boy chile and de very spit of you."

"You reckon, Missie May?"

"Who else could it look lak?"

Joe said nothing, but he thrust his hand deep into his pocket and fingered something there.

It was almost six months later Missie May took to bed and Joe went and got his mother to come wait on the house.

Missie May delivered a fine boy. Her travail was over when Joe came in from work one morning. His mother and the old women were drinking great bowls of coffee around the fire in the kitchen.

The minute Joe came into the room his mother called him aside.

"How did Missie May make out?" he asked quickly.

"Who, dat gal? She strong as a ox. She gointer have plenty

mo'. We done fixed her wid de sugar and lard to sweeten her for de nex' one."

Joe stood silent awhile.

"You ain't ast 'bout de baby, Joe. You oughter be mighty proud cause he sho' is de spittin' image of yuh, son. Dat's yourn all right, if you never git another one, dat un is yourn. And you know Ah'm mighty proud too, son, cause Ah never thought well of you marryin' Missie May cause her ma used tuh fan her foot 'round right smart and Ah been mighty skeered dat Missie May wuz gointer git misput on her road."

Joe said nothing. He fooled around the house till late in the day then just before he went to work, he went and stood at the foot of the bed and asked his wife how she felt. He did this every day during the week.

On Saturday he went to Orlando to make his market. It had been a long time since he had done that.

Meat and lard, meal and flour, soap and starch. Cans of corn and tomatoes. All the staples. He fooled around town for awhile and bought bananas and apples. Way after while he went around to the candy store.

"Hellow, Joe," the clerk greeted him. "Ain't seen you in a long time."

"Nope, Ah ain't been heah. Been 'round spots and places."

"Want some of them molasses kisses you always buy?"

"Yessuh." He threw the gilded half-dollar on the counter. "Will dat spend?"

"Whut is it, Joe? Well, I'll be doggone! A gold-plated four-bit piece. Where'd you git it, Joe?"

"Offen a stray nigger dat come through Eatonville. He had it on his watch chain for a charm — goin' 'round making out iss gold money. Ha ha! He had a quarter on his tie pin and it wuz all golded up too. Tryin' to fool people. Makin' out he so rich and everything. Ha! Ha! Tryin' to tole off folkses wives from home."

"How did you git it, Joe? Did he fool you, too?"

"Who, me? Naw suh! He ain't fooled me none. Know whut Ah done? He come 'round me wid his smart talk. Ah hauled off and knocked 'im down and took his old four-bits 'way from 'im. Gointer buy my wife some good ole 'lasses kisses wid it. Gimme fifty cents worth of dem candy kisses."

"Fifty cents buys a mightly lot of candy kisses, Joe. Why don't you split it up and take some chocolate bars, too. They eat good, too."

"Yessuh, dey do, but Ah wants all dat in kisses. Ah got a li'l boy chile home now. Tain't a week old yet, but he kin suck a sugar tit and maybe eat one them kisses hisself."

Joe got his candy and left the store. The clerk turned to the next customer. "Wisht I could be like these darkies. Laughin' all the time. Nothin' worries 'em."

Back in Eatonville, Joe reached his own front door. There was the ring of singing metal on wood. Fifteen times. Missie May couldn't run to the door, but she crept there as quickly as she could.

"Joe Banks, Ah hear you chunkin' money in mah do'way. You wait till Ah got mah strength back and Ah'm gointer fix you for dat."

C·O·C·K R·O·B·I·N
B·E·A·L·E S·T·R·E·E·T

UNCLE JULY WAS mad clear through. A'nt Dooby could tell by the way he threw down the load of kindling in the corner behind the kitchen stove. Anyhow, if he wasn't really mad, he was letting on like it. It was an off day with her and she didn't feel like no fussing, so she started in right away to head him off.

"July, don't you come in here starting none of your foolishness wid me this day and year of our Lawd! I done told you now!"

"Who's starting any fussing? I know tain't none of me. I ain't broke a breath wid you, 'oman. You better go 'head and leave me be."

A'nt Dooby braced herself for the storm. She plunked her fat fists on her abundant hips and glared him round the room. July could see names like 'mule' 'fool' 'sea-buzzard' 'groundhog' and things like that swimming around in her eyes. So he sat down, pulled off one shoe, looked at it hard, then pulled off the other one, wiggled his toes and lit his pipe.

"Hit's a sin before de living jestice!" July exploded. "Dese white folks ought to talk whut dey know, and testify to whut dey see."

"Whut's de matter now?" Dooby asked, full of suspicion.

"Going 'round letting on dat Cock Robin was a bird! Jest heard Miz Pendleton reading out of some kind of a book how Cock Robin was a real-true bird wid feathers on him and got kilt wid a arrow. Hit's a sin and shame! Tain't a word of it so! I knowed Cock Robin well—was right dere when he got kilt wid a forty-four, and was at de funeral."

A'nt Dooby was unimpressed.

"I ain't knowed nothing 'bout no Cock Robin gitting kilt and you must a' sneaked off to de funeral and never told me nothing 'tall about it."

"Oh, dat was back dere in Memphis. I used to git around right-smart before I was saved. Long before I and you made a wed. And den it wasn't exactly no funeral neither. Dere was some talk about funeralizing him, but it didn't amount to nothing. Cock Robin was a high-flier if ever I seed one. Sung in de choir, and got 'round right smart wid de lady-people. Comed to Memphis from off somewhere like a whole heap of us done. Big doings in Memphis in dem days.

"Well, late one evening just 'fore sundown everybody was down 'round Beale Street sort of catching de cool breezes off de gutter wid de Grease Spot doing a heap of business, de pool-room was full, and somebody was jooking on de piano in de Shimmy Shack, dat was a high class hotel run by Sister Buzzard, slap on Beale.

"Quite a few folks was scattered around de place upstairs and down, when all of suddent we heard three pistol shots down 'round de front. Everybody run to de street. Dere was Cock Robin laying on de sidewalk in front of de hotel wid three bullet holes in him.

"Brother Owl, he was around so he naturally took charge

and went to asking folks, 'Who kilt Cock Robin?' Not expecting to git much of a answer.

" 'I kilt Cock Robin,' Brother Sparrow says, pushing up front in de crowd. 'Who is it wants to know?' He had his gun wide open in his hand.

" 'Not dat we cares, Brother Sparrow', Brother Owl sort of simmerized, 'Us just asked for a little information to find out how come.'

" 'Well, it's like dis,' Brother Sparrow told him, and sort of reared back on his dew-claws. 'You all knows dat I am a sparrow, and all my folks was sparrows from way back.'

" 'Dat sho' is de truth,' they told him, 'De spitting image of your paw.'

" 'And furthermore, you all know dat sparrow don't never lay nothing but plain white eggs. My great-great-great grandma, she laid white eggs. My mama laid white eggs.'

" 'Dat sho' is de truth!' Sister Buzzard put in. 'Your maw and your paw did they nesting right here in my Shimmy Shack.'

" 'Well, now when me and my wife first started to nesting, she never laid nothing but plain white eggs. But things done changed, ever since dat Cock Robin been 'round here. Now, every time I go off on a worm hunt, when I get back, I find another blue egg in my nest.'

" 'Dere now!' Brother Crow hollered and jumped clear up in de air. 'You done got *me* to scratching where I don't itch. Seem like to me, I seen a bluish egg or two 'round my nest, too.'

" 'Tain't no ifs and ands about it,' Brother Bull snorted, 'Cock Robin was in de egg business. Whilst I sympathizes wid Brother Sparrow, I'm glad we don't have no egg-laying 'round our place.'

" 'You mean Cock Robin been laying eggs?' Brother Fly asked.

" 'Aw, naw! You know no rooster don't lay no eggs. Us leave things like dat to de hen-folks,' Brother Owl hooted. 'But he was too mixified just de same.'

" 'You done right, Brother Sparrow,' everybody told him. 'Kilt him in de first degree and finished de job off well.'

" 'All we got to do now is to funeralize him,' Brother Owl said and got him a high chair to sit on. 'He was sort of unfinancial, so we got to do 'round to fix things up.'

"Wid that, he took and 'signed different ones to do and to fix until he had a burial robe and everything fixed up down to de chief mourner which was Sister Dove. She was a widow 'oman and used to mourning, and she really could mourn. Den he took up de hall he was going to be funeralized from.

"Right dere was where he throwed de fat in de fire 'cause Brother Cock Robin belonged to every fraternal and benevolent society 'round dere. De Night-Stepping Owls allowed dat he was a brother in good standing, and naturally dey would parade him to de graveyard. De Never-Been-Caught Fishes, De Ever-Blooming Blackbirds, De Muckty-Duckty Beetle-Bugs, De High-Roosting Crows and Fun-Feeling Flies all hollered dat dey put on de best funerals in town. Dey argued, and went home and got into regalia to show Brother Owl how dey paraded, and brought along de bands and put de thing on. Brother Owl couldn't say for not knowing which one of dem was de best. Brother Bull, he stood dere by Brother Owl and said, 'I don't care who gits de deceasted. I aim to march in front.'

" 'How come, Brother Bull?' Dey all wanted to know. 'You don't belong to none of de orders.'

" 'Matters a difference about dat,' he told 'em. 'You know

dat bull goes in front of everythings. *I aims to march in front.* I got my parading stick all ready and my strutting hat.'

"Brother Owl scratched his head all over two or three more times and den he said, 'Everybody parades de best. So as not to have no hard feeling, who ever pays de funeral expenses can have de body. Dat's fair.'

"De unfairness of de thing took everybody by surprise, so nobody couldn't say a word for a long time. Finally, Sister Blackbird up and told him, 'Brother Owl, if you was talking about money all dis time, how come you never told nobody? Here you done got us all dressed up to funeralize our dear deceased, and now you come talking about money. My people! My people!'

" 'Yeah, and had us gitting up bands to march by and everything,' Sparrow told him. Everybody was good and mad at Brother Owl.

"Brother Crow snapped his fingers and said, 'Folkses and feathers, I clean forgot! Sister Speckled-Hen is having a big fish fry and barbecue down on Front Street and Beale dis evening. She told me to tell everybody, but all dis mess 'bout Cock Robin put it clean out of my head.' He rolled his eyes at Brother Owl. Everybody begin to get more lively right away, so Brother Crow went on. 'Since we is all 'sembled right here together, and in regalia, how come we don't all form one big amalgamated, contaminated parade down to Sister Speckled-Hen's place and enjoy de consequences?'

"Dat sounded like a good idea to everybody, so dey agreed all at one time. Nobody was de last. Brother Owl dusted hisself off and got ready. Brother Bull halted everthing until he got his strutting hat set over one eye so it looked like it couldn't stay on, but was just too mean to fall off. He whirled his parading stick and told de professor of de band to turn it on.

"But Sister Buzzard raised a rukus. Dey wasn't going to leave Cock Robin in front of *her* hotel, giving the place a bad name. Naw sir! Dey was going to take him up from dere and bury him.

"Feathers begin to crumple. Dey tried to make dis one and dat one do de burying, but everybody was otherwise engaged. 'Way after while Brother Owl told her, 'Oh, leave de white folks bury him! Dey always loves to take charge.'

"De band hit a hatful of notes at one lick, and Brother Bull lead off. Sister Speckled-Hen sho' done herself proud dat night. Lawd! I ain't never had dat much fun before nor since."

Uncle July looked kind of sheepish at Dooby. "Since I been saved, I forgot all about such doings. Never would have remembered it no more if dese white folks had of got de thing like it was sho' nuff."

"Humph!" A'nt Dooby snorted. "Old coon for cunning; young coon for running. Now tell me whut you done wid your wages. I know you been up to something. Tell me! You and your Muckty-Duckty Beetle-Bugs!"

B·O·O·K
O·F H·A·R·L·E·M

1. A pestilence visiteth the land of Hokum, and the people cry out. 4. Toothsome, a son of Georgia returns from Babylon, and stirreth up the Hamites. 10. Mandolin heareth him and resolveth to see Babylon. 11. He convinceth his father and departs for Babylon. 21. A red-cap toteth his bag, and uttereth blasphemy against Mandolin. 26. He lodgeth with Toothsome, and trieth to make the females of Harlem, but is scorned by them. 28. One frail biddeth him sit upon a tack. 29. He taketh council with Toothsome and is comforted. 33. He goeth to an hall of dancing, and meeting a damsel there, shaketh vehemently with her. 42. He discloseth himself to her and she telleth him what to read. 49. He becometh Panic. 50. The Book of Harlem.

1. AND IN THOSE DAYS when King Volstead sat upon the throne in Hokum, then came a mighty drought upon the land, many cried out in agony thereof.

2. Then did the throat parch and the tongue was thrust into the cheek of many voters.

3. And men grew restless and went up and down in the land

saying, "We are verily the dry-bones of which the prophet Ezekiel prophesied."

4. Then returned one called Toothsome unto his town of Standard Bottom, which is in the province of Georgia. And he was of the tribe of Ham.

5. And his raiment was very glad, for he had sojourned in the city of Babylon, which is ruled by the tribe of Tammany. And his garments putteth out the street lamps, and the vaseline upon his head, yea verily the slickness thereof did outshine the sun at noonday.

6. And the maidens looked upon him and were glad, but the men gnasheth together their bridgework at sight of him. But they drew near unto him and listened to his accounts of the doings of Babylon, for they all yearned unto that city.

7. And the mouth of Toothsome flapped loudly and fluently in the marketplace, and the envy of his hearers increased an hundredfold.

8. Then stood one youth before him, and his name was called Mandolin. And he questioned Toothsome eagerly, asking 'how come' and 'wherefore' many times.

9. And Toothsome answered him according to his wit. Moreover he said unto the youth, "Come thou also to the city as unto the ant, and consider her ways and be wise."

10. And the heart of Mandolin was inflamed, and he stood before his father and said, "I beseech thee now, papa, to give unto me now my portion that I may go hence to great Babylon and see life."

11. But his father's heart yearned towards him, and he said, "Nay, my son, for Babylon is full of wickedness, and thou art but a youth."

12. But Mandolin answered him saying, "I crave to gaze upon its sins. What do you think I go to see, a prayer-meeting?"

13. But his father strove with him and said, "Why dost thou crave Babylon when Gussie Smith, the daughter of our neighbor, will make thee a good wife? Tarry now and take her to wife, for verily she is a mighty biscuit cooker before the Lord."

14. Then snorted Mandolin with scorn and he said, "What care I for biscuit-cookers when there be Shebas of high voltage on every street in Harlem? For verily man liveth not by bread alone, but by every drop of banana oil that drippeth from the tongue of the lovely."

15. Then strove they together all night. But at daybreak did Mandolin touch the old man upon the hip, yea verily upon the pocket-bearing joint, and triumphed.

16. So the father gave him his blessing, and he departed out of Standard Bottom on his journey to Babylon.

17. And he carried with him of dreams forty-and-four thousands, and of wishes ten thousands, and of hopes ten thousands.

18. But of tears or sorrows carried he none out of all that land. Neither bore he any fears away with him.

19. And journeyed he many days upon the caravan of steel, and came at last unto the city of Babylon, and got him down within the place.

20. Then rushed there many upon him who wore scarlet caps upon the head, saying "Porter? Shall I tote thy bags for thee?"

21. And he marvelled greatly within himself, saying, "How charitably are the Babylons, seeing they permit no stranger to tote his own bag! With what great kindness am I met!"

22. And he suffered one to prevail and tote his bag for him. Moreover he questioned him concerning the way to Harlem which is a city of Ham in Babylonia.

23. And when he of the scarlet cap had conducted Mandolin unto a bus, then did Mandolin shake hands with him and thank him greatly for his kindness, and stepped upon the chariot as it

rolled away, and took his way unto Harlem.

24. Then did the bag-toter blaspheme greatly, saying, "Oh, the cock-eyed son of a wood louse! Oh, the hawg! Oh, the sea-buzzard! Oh, the splay-footed son of a doodle bug and cockroach! What does he take me for? The mule's daddy! The clod-hopper! If only I might lay my hands upon him, verily would I smite him, yea, until he smelt like onions!"

25. But Mandolin journeyed on to Harlem, knowing none of these things.

26. And when he had come unto the place, he lodged himself with Toothsome, and was glad.

27. And each evening stood he before the Lafayette theatre and a-hemmed at the knees that passed, but none took notice of him.

28. Moreover one frail of exceeding sassiness bade him go to and cook an radish, and seat himself upon a tack, which being interpreted is slander.

29. Then went he unto his roommate and saith, "How now doth the damsel think me? Have I not a smiling countenance, and coin in my jeans? My heart is heavy for I have sojourned in Harlem for many weeks, but as yet I have spoken to no female."

30. Then spoke Toothsome, and answered him saying, "Seek not swell Shebas in mail-order britches. Go thou into the marketplace and get thee Oxford bags and jacket thyself likewise. Procure thee shoes and socks. Yea, anoint thy head with oil until it runneth over so that thou dare not hurl thyself into bed unless thou wear Weed chains upon the head, lest thou skid out again."

31. "Moreover lubricate thy tongue with banana oil, for from the oily lips proceedeth the breath of love."

32. And Mandolin hastened to do all that his counsellor bade him.

33. Then hied him to the hall of dancing where many leaped with the cymbal, and shook with the drums.

34. And his belly was moved, for he saw young men seize upon damsels and they stood upon the floor and 'messed around' meanly. Moreover many 'bumped' them vehemently. Yea, there were those among them who shook with many shakings.

35. And when he saw all these things, Mandolin yearned within his heart to do likewise, but as yet he had spoken to no maiden.

36. But one damsel of scarlet lips smiled broadly upon him, and encouraged him with her eyes, and the water of his knees turned to bone, and he drew nigh unto her.

37. And his mouth flew open and he said, "See now how the others do dance with the cymbal and harp, yea, even the saxophone? Come thou and let us do likewise."

38. And he drew her and they stood upon the floor. Now this maiden was a mighty dancer before the Lord; yea, of the mightiest of all the tribe of Ham. And the shakings of the others was as one stricken with paralysis beside a bowl of gelatine. And the heart of the youth leaped for joy.

39. And he was emboldened, and his mouth flew open and the banana oil did drip from his lips, yea even down to the floor, and the maiden was moved.

40. And he said, "Thou sure art propaganda! Yea, verily thou shakest a wicked ankle."

41. And she being pleased, answered him, "Thou art some sheik thyself. I do shoot a little pizen to de ankle if I do say so myself. Where has thou been all my life that I have not seen thee?"

42. Then did his mouth fly open, and he told her everything of

Standard Bottom, Georgia, and of Babylon, and of all those things which touched him.

43. And her heart yearned towards him, and she resolved to take him unto herself and to make him wise.

44. And she said unto him, "Go thou and buy the books and writings of certain scribes and Pharisees which I shall name unto you, and thou shalt learn everything of good and of evil. Yea, thou shalt know as much as the Chief of the Niggerati, who is called Carl Van Vechten."

45. And Mandolin diligently sought all these books and writings that he was bidden, and read them.

46. Then was he sought for all feasts, and stomps, and shakings, and none was complete without him. Both on 139th street and on Lenox avenue was he sought, and his fame was great.

47. And his name became Panic, for they asked one of the other, "Is he not a riot in all that he doeth?"

48. Then did he devise poetry, and played it upon the piano, saying:

> *Skirt by skirt on every flirt*
> *They're getting higher and higher*
> *Day by day in every way*
> *There's more to admire*
> *Sock by sock and knee by knee*
> *The more they show, the more we see*
> *The skirts run up, the socks run down*
> *Jingling bells run round and round*
> *Oh week by week, and day by day*
> *Let's hope that things keep on this way*
> *Let's kneel right down and pray.*

49. And the women all sought him, and damsels and the

matrons and the grandmothers and all those who wear the skirt, and with them his name was continually Panic.

50. Of his doings and success after that, is it not written in The Book of Harlem?

S·T·O·R·Y I·N
H·A·R·L·E·M S·L·A·N·G

Jelly's Tale

WAIT TILL I light up my coal-pot and I'll tell you about this Zigaboo called Jelly. Well, all right now. He was a sealskin brown and papa-tree-top tall. Skinny in the hips and solid built for speed. He was born with this rough-dried hair, but when he laid on the grease and pressed it down overnight with his stocking-cap, it looked just like that righteous moss, and had so many waves you got seasick from looking. Solid, man, solid!

His mama named him Marvel, but after a month on Lenox Avenue, he changed all that to Jelly. How come? Well, he put it in the street that when it came to filling that long-felt need, sugar-curing the ladies' feelings, he was in a class by himself and nobody knew his name, so he had to tell 'em. "It must be jelly, 'cause jam don't shake." Therefore, his name was Jelly. That was what was on his sign. The stuff was there and it was mellow. Whenever he was challenged by a hard-head or a frail eel on the right of his title he would eyeball the idol-breaker with a slice of ice and put on his ugly-laugh, made up of scorn and pity, and say: "Youse just dumb to the fact, baby. If you don't know what you talking 'bout, you better ask Granny

Grunt. I wouldn't mislead you, baby. I don't need to — not with the help I got." Then he would give the pimp's sign* and percolate on down the Avenue. You can't go behind a fact like that.

So this day he was airing out on the Avenue. It had to be late afternoon, or he would not have been out of bed. All you did by rolling out early was to stir your stomach up. That made you hunt for more dishes to dirty. The longer you slept, the less you had to eat. But you can't collar nods all day. No matter how long you stay in bed, and how quiet you keep, sooner or later that big gut is going to reach over and grab that little one and start to gnaw. That's confidential right from the Bible. You got to get out on the beat and collar yourself a hot.

So Jelly got into his zoot suit with the reet pleats and got out to skivver around and do himself some good. At 132nd Street, he spied one of his colleagues on the opposite sidewalk, standing in front of a cafe. Jelly figured that if he bull-skated just right, he might confidence Sweet Back out of a thousand on a plate. Maybe a shot of scrap-iron or a reefer. Therefore, Jelly took a quick backward look at his shoe soles to see how his leather was holding out. The way he figured it after the peep was that he had plenty to get across and maybe do a little more cruising besides. So he stanched out into the street and made the crossing.

"Hi there, Sweet Back!" he exploded cheerfully. "Gimme some skin!"

"Lay de skin on me, pal!" Sweet Back grabbed Jelly's

---

*In Harlemese, *pimp* has a different meaning than its ordinary definition as a procurer for immoral purposes. The Harlem pimp is a man whose amatory talents are for sale to any woman who will support him, either with a free meal or on a common law basis; in this sense, he is actually a male prostitute.

outstretched hand and shook hard. "Ain't seen you since the last time, Jelly. What's cookin'?"

"Oh, just like de bear—I ain't nowhere. Like de bear's brother, I ain't no further. Like de bear's daughter—ain't got a quarter."

Right away, he wished he had not been so honest. Sweet Back gave him a top-superior, cut-eye look. Looked at Jelly just like a showman looks at an ape. Just as far above Jelly as fried chicken is over branch water.

"Cold in hand, hunh?" He talked down to Jelly. "A red hot pimp like you say you is, ain't got no business in the barrel. Last night when I left you, you was beating up your gums and broadcasting about how hot you was. Just as hot as July jam, you told me. What you doing cold in hand?"

"Aw, man, can't you take a joke? I was just beating up my gums when I said I was broke. How can I be broke when I got de best woman in Harlem? If I ask her for a dime, she'll give me a ten dollar bill; ask her for drink of likker, and she'll buy me a whiskey still. If I'm lying, I'm flying!"

"Gar, don't hang out dat dirty washing in my back yard! Didn't I see you last night with dat beat chick, scoffing a hot dog? Dat chick you had was beat to de heels. Boy, you ain't no good for what you live."

"If you ain't lying now, you flying. You ain't got de first thin. You ain't got nickel one."

Jelly threw back the long skirt of his coat and rammed his hand down into his pants pocket. "Put your money where your mouth is!" he challenged, as he mock-struggled to haul out a huge roll. "Back your crap with your money. I bet you five dollars!"

Sweet Back made the same gesture of hauling out non-existent money.

"I been raised in the church. I don't bet, but I'll doubt you. Five rocks!"

"I thought so!" Jelly crowed, and hurriedly pulled his empty hand out of his pocket. "I knowed you'd back up when I drawed my roll on you."

"You ain't drawed no roll on me, Jelly. You ain't drawed nothing but your pocket. You better stop dat boogerbooing. Next time I'm liable to make you do it." There was a splinter of regret in his voice. If Jelly really had had some money, he might have staked him, Sweet Back, to a hot. Good Southern cornbread with a piano on a platter. Oh, well! The right broad would, or might, come along.

"Who boogerbooing?" Jelly snorted. "Jig, I don't have to. Talking about *me* with a beat chick scoffing a hot dog! You must of not seen me, 'cause last night I was riding 'round in a Yellow Cab, with a yellow gal, drinking yellow likker and spending yellow money. Tell 'em 'bout me, tell 'em!"

"Git out of my face, Jelly! Dat broad I seen you with wasn't no pe-ola. She was one of them coal-scuttle blondes with hair just as close to her head as ninety-nine is to a hundred. She look-ted like she had seventy-five pounds of clear bosom, guts in her feet, and she look-ted like six months in front and nine months behind. Buy you a whiskey still! Dat broad couldn't make the down payment on a pair of sox."

"Sweet Back, you fixing to talk out of place." Jelly stiffened.

"If you trying to jump salty, Jelly, that's your mammy."

"Don't play in de family, Sweet Back. I don't play de dozens. I done told you."

"Who? Me? Long as you been knowing me, Sweet Back, you ain't never seen me with nothing but pe-olas. I can get any frail eel I wants to. How come I'm up here in New York? You don't know, do you? Since youse dumb to the fact, I reckon I'll have to make you hep. I had to leave from down south 'cause Miss Anne used to worry me so bad to go with me. Who, me? Man, I don't deal in no coal. Know what I tell 'em? If they's yellow, they's mellow! If they's brown, they can stick around. But if they come black, they better git way back! Tell 'em 'bout me!"

"Aw, man, you trying to show your grandma how to milk ducks. Best you can do is to confidence some kitchen-mechanic out of a dime or two. Me, I knocks de pad with them cack-broads up on Sugar Hill, and fills 'em full of melody. Man, I'm quick death and easy judgment. Youse just a home-boy, Jelly. Don't try to follow me."

"Me follow *you*! man, I come on like the Gang Busters, and go off like The March of Time! If dat ain't so, God is gone to Jersey City and you know He wouldn't be messing 'round a place like that. Know what my woman done? We hauled off and went to church last Sunday, and when they passed 'round the plate for the *penny* collection, I throwed in a dollar. De man looked at me real hard for dat. Dat made my woman mad, so she called him back and throwed in a twenty dollar bill! Told him to take dat and go! Dat's what he got for looking at me 'cause I throwed in a dollar."

"Jelly, de wind may blow and de door may slam; dat what you shooting ain't worth a damn!"

Jelly slammed his hand in his bosom as if to draw a gun. Sweet Back did the same.

"If you wants to fight, Sweet Back, the favor is in me."

"I was deep-thinking then, Jelly. It's a good thing I ain't short-tempered. Tain't nothing to you, nohow. You ain't hit me yet."

Both burst into a laugh and changed from fighting to lounging poses.

"Don't get too yaller on me, Jelly. You liable to get hurt some day."

"You over-sports your hand you ownself. Too blamed astorperious. I just don't pay you no mind. Lay de skin on me!"

They broke their handshake hurriedly, because both of them looked up the Avenue and saw the same thing. It was a girl and they both remembered that it was Wednesday afternoon. All of the domestics off for the afternoon with their pay in their pockets. Some of them bound to be hungry for love. That meant a dinner, a shot of scrap-iron, maybe room rent and a reefer or two. Both went into the pose and put on the look.

"Big stars falling!" Jelly said out loud when she was in hearing distance. "It must be just before day!"

"Yeah, man!" Sweet Back agreed. "Must be a recess in Heaven — pretty angel like that out on the ground."

The girl drew abreast of them, reeling and rocking her hips.

"I'd walk clear to Diddy-Wah-Diddy to get a chance to speak to a pretty li'l ground-angel like that," Jelly said.

"Aw, man, you ain't willing to go very far. Me, I'd go slap to Ginny-Gall, where they eat cow-rump, skin and all."

The girl smiled, so Jelly set his hat and took the plunge.

"Baby," he crooned, "what's on de rail for de lizard?"

The girl halted and braced her hips with her hands. "A Zigaboo down in Georgy, where I come from, asked a woman that one time and the judge told him ninety days."

"Georgy!" Sweet Back pretended to be elated. "Where 'bouts in Georgy is you from? Delaware?"

"Delaware?" Jelly snorted. "My people! My people! Free schools and dumb jigs! Man, how you going to put Delaware in Georgy? You ought to know dat's in Maryland."

"Oh, don't try to make out youse no northerner, you! Youse

from right down in 'Bam your ownself!" The girl turned on
Jelly.

"Yeah, I'm *from* there and I aims to stay from there."

"One of them Russians, eh?" The girl retorted. "Rushed
up here to get away from a job of work."

That kind of talk was not leading towards the dinner table.

"But baby!" Jelly gasped. "Dat shape you got on you! I bet
the Coca Cola Company is paying you good money for the
patent!"

The girl smiled with pleasure at this, so Sweet Back jumped
in.

"I know youse somebody swell to know. Youse real people.
You grins like a regular fellow." He gave her his most killing
look and let it simmer in. "There dickty jigs round here tries
to smile. S'pose you and me go inside the café here and grab a
hot?"

"You got any money?" The girl asked, and stiffed like a
ramrod. "Nobody ain't pimping on me. You dig me?"

"Aw, now, baby!"

"I seen you two mullet-heads before. I was uptown when
Joe Brown had you all in the go-long last night. Dat cop sure
hates a pimp! All he needs to see is the pimps' salute and he'll
out with his night-stick and ship your head to the red. Beat
your head just as flat as a dime!" She went off into a great blow
of laughter.

"Oh, let's us don't talk about the law. Let's talk about us,"
Sweet Back persisted. "You going inside with me to holler 'let
one come flopping! One come grunting! Snatch one from de
rear!"

"Naw indeed!" the girl laughed harshly. "You skillets is
trying to promote a meal on me. But it'll never happen, brother.
You barking up the wrong tree. I wouldn't give you air if you

was stopped up in a jug. I'm not putting out a thing. I'm just
like the cemetery — I'm not putting out, I'm taking in! Dig?"

"I'll tell you like the farmer told the potato — plant you now
and dig you later."

The girl made a movement to switch on off. Sweet Back had
not dirtied a plate since the day before. He made a weak but
desperate gesture.

"Trying to snatch my pocketbook, eh?" She blazed. Instead
of running, she grabbed hold of Sweet Back's draping coat-tail
and made a slashing gesture. "How much split you want back
here? If your feets don't hurry up and take you 'way from here,
you'll *ride* away. I'll spread my lungs all over New York and call
the law. Go ahead. Bedbug! Touch me! And I'll holler like a
pretty white woman!"

The boys were ready to flee, but she turned suddenly and
rocked on off with her earring snapping and her heels popping.

"My people! My people!" Sweet Back sighed.

"I know you feel chewed," Jelly said, in an effort to make it
appear that he had had no part in the fiasco.

"Oh, let her go," Sweet Back said magnanimously. "When
I see people without the periodical principles they's supposed
to have, I just don't fool with 'em. What I want to steal her old
pocketbook with all the money I got? I could buy a beat chick
like her and give her away. I got money's mammy and Grandma
change. One of my women, and not the best one I got neither,
is buying me ten shag suits at one time."

He glanced sidewise at Jelly to see if he was convincing. But
Jelly's thoughts were far away. He was remembering those full,
hot meals he had left back in Alabama to seek wealth and
splendor in Harlem without working. He had even forgotten
to look cocky and rich.

GLOSSARY OF HARLEM SLANG

Air out — *leave, flee, stroll*
Astorperious — *haughty, biggity*
Aunt Hagar — *Negro race* (also Aunt Hagar's chillun)
Bad hair — *Negro type hair*
Balling — *having fun*
'Bam, *and* down in 'Bam — *down South*
Battle-hammed — *badly formed about the hips*
Beating up your gums — *talking to no purpose*
Beluthahatchie — *next station beyond Hell*
Big boy — *stout fellow. But in the South, it means fool and is a prime insult.*
Blowing your top — *getting very angry; occasionally used to mean, "He's doing fine!"*
Boogie-woogie — *type of dancing and rhythm. For years, in the South, it meant secondary syphilis.*
Brother-in-black — *Negro*
Bull-skating — *Bragging*
Butt sprung — *a suit or a skirt out of shape in the rear*
Coal scuttle blonde — *black woman*
Cold — *exceeding, well, etc., as in "He was cold on that trumpet!"*
Collar a nod — *sleep*

Collar a hot — *eat a meal*

Color scale — *high yaller, yaller, high brown, vaseline brown, seal brown, low brown, dark black*

Conk buster — *cheap liquor; also an intellectual Negro*

Cruising — *parading down the Avenue. Variations:* oozing, percolating, *and* free-wheeling. *The latter implies more briskness.*

Cut — *doing something well*

Dark black — *a casually black person. Superlatives:* low black, *a blacker person;* lam black, *still blacker; and* damn black, *blackest man, of whom it is said:* "Why, lightning bugs follows him at 12 o'clock in the day, thinking it's midnight."

Dat thing — *sex of either sex*

Dat's your mammy — *same as,* "So is your old man."

Diddy-Wah-Diddy — *a far place, a measure of distance. (2) another suburb of Hell, built since way before Hell wasn't no bigger than Baltimore. The folks in Hell go there for a big time.*

Dig — *understand.* "Dig me?" *means,* "Do you get me? Do you collar the jiver?"

Draped down — *dressed in the height of Harlem fashion; also* togged down.

Dumb to the fact — "You don't know what you're talking about."

Dusty butt — *cheap prostitute*

Eight-rock — *very black person*

Every postman on his beat — *kinky hair*

First thing smoking — *a train.* "I'm through with this town. I mean to grab the first thing smoking."

Frail eel — *pretty girl*

Free schools — *a shortened expression of deprecation derived from* "free schools and dumb Negroes," *sometimes embellished with* "free schools, pretty yellow teachers and dumb Negroes."

Function — *a small, unventilated dance, full of people too casually bathed*

Gator-faced — *long, black face with big mouth*

Getting on some stiff time — *really doing well with your racket*

Get you to go — *power, physical or otherwise, to force the opponent to run*

Ginny Gall — *a suburb of Hell, a long way off*

Git up off of me — *quit talking about me, leave me alone*

Go when the wagon comes — *another way of saying, "You may be acting biggity now, but you'll cool down when enough power gets behind you."*

Good hair — *Caucasian-type hair*

Granny Grunt — *a mythical character to whom most questions may be referred*

Ground rations — *sex, also under rations*

Gum beater — *a blowhard, a braggart, idle talker in general*

Gut-bucket — *low dive, type of music, or expression from same*

Gut-foot — *bad case of fallen arches*

Handkerchief-head — *sycophant type of Negro; also an Uncle Tom*

Hauling — *fleeing on foot. "Man! He cold hauled it!"*

I don't deal in coal — *"I don't keep company with black women."*

I'm cracking but I'm facking — *"I'm wisecracking, but I'm telling the truth."*

Inky dink — *very black person*

I shot him lightly and he died politely — *"I completely outdid him."*

Jar head — *Negro man*

Jelly — *sex*

Jig — *Negro, a corrupted shortening of Zigaboo*

Jook — *a pleasure house, in the class of gut-bucket; now common all over the South*

Jooking — *playing the piano, guitar, or any musical instrument in the manner of the Jooks (pronounced like "took") (2) dancing and 'scronching', ditto*

Juice — *liquor*

July jam — *something very hot*

Jump salty — *get angry*

Kitchen mechanic — *a domestic*

Knock yourself out — *have a good time*

Lightly, slightly and politely — *doing things perfectly*

Little sister — *measure of hotness: "Hot as little sister!"*

Liver-lip — *pendulous, thick purple lips*

Made hair — *hair that has been straightened*

Mammy — *a term of insult. Never used in any other way by Negroes.*

Miss Anne — *a white woman*

Mister Charlie — *a white man*

Monkey chaser — *a West Indian*

Mug Man — *small-time thug or gangster*

My people! My people! — *Sad and satiric expression in the Negro language; sad when a Negro comments on the backwardness of some members of his race; at other times, used for satiric or comic effect.*

Naps — *kinky hair*

Nearer my God to Thee — *good hair*

Nothing to the bear but his curly hair — *"I call your bluff," or "Don't be afraid of him; he won't fight."*

Now you cookin' with gas — *now you're talking, in the groove, etc.*

Ofay — *white person*

Old cuffee — *Negro (genuine African word for the same thing)*

Palmer House — *walking flat-footed, as from fallen arches*

Pancake — *a humble type of Negro*

Park ape — *an ugly, underprivileged Negro*

Peckerwood — *poor and unloved class of Southern whites*

Peeping through my likkers — *carrying on even though drunk*

Pe-ola — *a very white Negro girl*

Piano — *spare ribs (white rib-bones suggest piano keys)*

Pig meat — *young girl*

Pilch — *house or apartment; residence*

Pink toes — *yellow girl*

Playing the dozens — *low-rating the ancestors of your opponent*

Red neck — *poor Southern white man*

Reefer — *marijuana cigarette, also* a drag

Righteous mass or grass — *good hair*

Righteous rags — *the components of a Harlem-style suit*

Rug-cutter — *originally a person frequenting house-rent parties, cutting up the rugs of the host with his feet; a person too cheap or poor to patronize regular dance halls; now means a good dancer.*

Russian — *a Southern Negro up north. "Rushed up here," hence a Russian.*

Scrap iron — *cheap liquor*

Sell out — *run in fear*

Sender — *he or she who can get you to go, i.e., has what it takes. Used often as a compliment: "He's a solid sender!"*

Smoking, *or* smoking over — *looking someone over*

Solid — *perfect*

Sooner — *anything cheap and mongrel, now applied to cheap clothes, or a shabby person*

Stanch, or stanch out — *to begin, commence, step out*

Stomp — *low dance, "but hat man!"*

Stormbuzzard — *shiftless, homeless character*

Stroll — *doing something well*

Sugar Hill — *northwest sector of Harlem, near Washington Heights, site of the newest apartment houses, mostly occupied by professional people. (The expression has been distorted in the South to mean a Negro red light district.)*

The bear — *confession of poverty*

The big apple, *also* the big red apple — *New York City*

The man — *the law, or powerful boss*

Thousand on a plate — *beans*

Tight head — *one with kinky hair*

Trucking — *strolling. (2) dance step from the strolling motif*

V and X — *five-and-ten-cent store*

West Hell — *another suburb of Hell, worse than the original*

What's on the rail for the lizard? — *suggestion for moral turpitude*

Whip it to the red — *beat your head until it is bloody*

Woofing — *aimless talk, as a dog barks on a moonless night*

Young suit — *ill-fitting, too small. Observers pretend to believe you're breaking in your little brother's suit for him.*

Your likker told you — *misguided behavior*

Zigaboo — *a Negro*

Zoot suit with the reet pleat — *Harlem style suit, padded shoulders, 43-inch trousers at the knee with cuff so small it needs a zipper to get into, high waistline, fancy lapels, bushels of buttons, etc.*

APPENDIX

Herod on Trial

While Sextus Caesar dictated his heated letter of protest to the high priest, Hyrcanus, Herod left word that he was going to visit the bazaars of Damascus, which were varied, and rich in merchandise. As always Herod was enchanted with the offerings and the shops of the various workers in precious metals and the lapidaries. How skilled were these men! Remembering his wife, Doris, Herod ordered anklets of fine gold adorned with sapphires and tinkling little bells. Then a necklace and bracelet to match. He bought six lengths of the richest silk, each a different color, and a flask of rare perfume brought all the way from China. For himself, Herod ordered sandals of gold leather with three straps that brought the top of the sandal up to his lower calf.

The stroll through Damascus lifted Herod's spirits. He admired again the ranging hills to the north of the city, the ancient highways, where it appeared that caravans from far places were forever approaching, bringing rich and rare objects, or, where caravans might also be departing to distant lands which Herod still yearned to see.

Later in the day Herod briefly visited the university where he had been educated. He warmly saluted his former instructors.

Soon Herod was surrounded by cheering crowds of students who honoured him as the conqueror of Hezekiah, as Governor of Galilee, and as the personal friend of Sextus Caesar. Soon a tall figure burst forward from an adjacent classroom, and threw himself at Herod.

"Nicolaus!" Herod cried. "Nicolaus, my classmate and my friend!"

"Herod! What brings you to Damascus? We hear of your exploits. Your glorious actions fill the world with news of your fame."

"The story can not be told in an instant, Nicolaus. Can you take leave? Can you accompany me back to the palace of the Governor?"

"Certainly," Nicolaus replied.

Along the way Herod told his intimate friend of his most recent adventures, and Nicolaus explained in turn why he had remained at the university.

"I have fallen in love with history, Herod, and I intend to become an able and truthful historian. So I am now absorbing the materials and the methods of recording history."

When they arrived together back at the palace, Sextus Caesar received Herod's friend graciously, and invited him to attend the banquet which was just then beginning. As they took their places, Caesar remarked generously, "This is a most unique occasion. On the one hand Herod seems unable to avoid making history, and you prepare to set it down. Excellent!"

"I may have made history in the past," Herod smiled, "yet certain holy men in Jerusalem seem bent on preventing me from making any more."

The three men laughed at this, then Sextus read his letter to Hyrcanus, and the other holy men concerned.

"It has come to my ears that, in association with the other so-called holy men at Jerusalem, you have summoned Herod, Governor of Galilee, and charged him with murder for exterminating the notorious bandit-leader, Hezekiah. I, Sextus Caesar, President of Syria by command of the Great Caesar and the Roman Senate, demand to know by what right you attempt such an audacious and insolent action.

"Under the decree of Caesar and the Roman Senate, all powers of the government are vested in our Consul, Antipater, made Procurator by Caesar. Nothing was left in your power except the exercise of your temple rites, and that power was extended only at the pleading of Antipater, your faithful friend, whose eminent son you now contrive to sentence to murder for simply performing great service to Rome, and to this Empire. Even you, as weak of mind as you have become, must understand that there could never be real peace and security if outlaws such as this Hezekiah could not be sought out, and punished.

"Why have you stood silent in the past in the face of Hezekiah's crime? And now, when Herod, at great peril to his life, has struck down this most certain criminal, why do you seek to rob Herod not only of his life, but of his glorious reputation as well?

"I accuse you further of not only attempting to murder Herod, under a most clumsy pretext, but also of planning to murder his father, the noble and eminent Antipater, which charge amounts to nothing less then sedition against Rome, as Antipater is our representative here in Palestine.

"I order you then to dismiss this foolish and wicked plan instantly. I order you to stand down on your charges against Herod when he finally arrives back in Jerusalem to stand his trial. If this is not done, I, as the representative of Rome in Syria, shall visit a terrible punishment upon you for daring to take into your hands rights and powers which you no longer possess, your government now being subject to the rule of Rome. Rome has chosen to place this local government in the hands of Antipater. Any attempt on your part, or the part of your fellow holy men, to usurp or overthrow that power will be regarded as a revolt against Rome itself, and Rome will respond accordingly."

Sextus looked up from the scroll, and queried Herod with his eyes.

"My father, Antipater, has tried to work with these priests," Herod said, somewhat reluctantly. "He has underestimated their motives, and overlooked their crimes, and their trickery. Hyrcanus was once my father's friend, and for my father, fidelity in friendship is a religion. I was taught as much as a child. And yet I have also learned that when a man has given me his right hand, and then plots against me like an enemy, friendship is no longer at stake. My father seems to be unable to see this low, cunning Hyrcanus as he really is. But a time will come when I shall have to pay him well for the treachery he has unleashed both to myself, and to my generous and innocent father as well."

"And my eminent cousin, Julius Caesar, will support your actions; for if ever there is a man whom Caesar loves, it is Antipater," Sextus Caesar exclaimed.

"That is all I require, O my kind friend," Herod replied. "Some day I shall certainly call this bumbling degenerate to accounts."

"Excellent! Now as to this present case, go to Jerusalem when you see fit. I see no necessity for haste, since there is some very good hunting and other sport in this area, and we must enjoy them together. Perhaps Nicolaus, your old friend, will also come along. And next week a troupe of very famous dancers from the Decapolis will also visit . . . we must not miss that . . . "

"And some excellent wrestlers from Macedonia," Nicolaus broke in with enthusiasm.

Sextus smiled, welcoming a new enthusiast.

"That is, Herod, if your affairs in Galilee can wait that long?"

"Certainly, Caesar. The elders in my territory are most able men. They look upon me as a son, and take pride in seeing our plans carried out."

"Well that is a triumph of administration, Herod," Sextus said. "I tell you that you have the qualities of a king. When the people come to enjoy supporting your measures, you have realized the genius of good government. But as for Jerusalem—when you *do* finally appear before Hyrcanus, you must do so in the full powers of your office . . . "

"Then perhaps, good Sextus," Herod smiled, "I will finally have occasion to wear the purple vestments you once bestowed on me."

This provoked loud laughter. "The very thing!" Sextus cried. Appear then in royal purple, your hair carefully barbered, and wear your most expensive and costly ornaments. Look like a king, Herod. The very sight of you dressed as such will throw that collection of old quacking geese into a whirl."

Caesar snickered, and continued, "I really would like to be there when you arrive. I am sure the sight would outdo the amphitheatre."

*

In Jerusalem, the tension mounted over Herod's forthcoming trial. Among Herod's enemies, the odds were ten to one he would be beheaded before sunset on the day he returned. The high priests walked about with smug smiles. The widows of Hezekiah's bandit gang were seen everywhere now, well-dressed, and boasting that Herod would soon pay with his head for destroying their husbands. As for Hyrcanus, he was already acting as if he were absolute monarch, his power unchallenged now, supreme.

"Herod is coming!" Crowds raced along the sidewalks, trying to keep pace with Herod's stallion as it picked proudly across the Valley of the Cheesemongers and upwards towards the Upper

Market Place. "Herod is coming. Hail valiant Herod!"

Inside the Hall of Justice the high priests stood about in small groups, speaking in low tones. At the cries from the street, they quietly took their places in the wide semi-circle. Hyrcanus moved in a pace between a swagger and a dodder as men often do, indicating the gap between the goal and the accomplishment. Reaching the seat in the center of the semi-circle, Hyrcanus stood for a moment, trying to awe the spectators before he sat down. He gave several wiggles of his hips, the better to sit before he went absolutely motionless.

"The old idiot is acting out what he conceives as being kingly behavior today," one spectator observed to his neighbor, "when all he achieves is the appearance of an old fussy hen returning to her nest. He even thinks his behind is royalty."

Those who overheard the spectator sniggered quietly. But their eyes were glued to the wide door for the first sight of Herod.

"Herod is near. I can make out the tread of many horses. Listen! Yes, horses. Many horses. But where is Herod's father? Has he been secretly murdered?"

The question was immediately answered. The young and handsome governor of Jerusalem entered with a bodyguard of no more than a dozen men, and he took his seat three rows from the front. As soon as he was seated, in came the Procurator of Judea with twenty-five men as his guards. He stood for the mighty ovation, smiled and lifted his right hand in salute to the people, and then seated himself in the front row with his guards disposed in a way to protect him.

An embarrassed silence fell on the platform as Antipater seated himself. Several of the seventy high priests rehearsed the speeches of indictment they would make, and the supreme moment when they would cast the condemning vote. Self-styled Ciceros bloomed all around the semi-circle. Hyrcanus rehearsed his sentencing speech with soundlessly moving lips.

"Herod is mounting the hill!" Jerusalem followed and cried out. Shopkeepers abandoned their shops recklessly; shoemakers ran away, some with their customers' shoes still clasped in their hands; women hung from windows; the rabble cried, and ran on.

Herod and his horsemen had to proceed with care now lest they trample the tumult down. Toothless old crones fought fiercely for a foothold in the rush and crush. The weak were elbowed aside.

Followed by his armed guard of two hundred and fifty men, Herod began to mount the stairs. The sound could be heard for miles. The priests took up a solemn and dignified look. None turned a head as the firm footsteps reached the landing, and approached the wide door.

Herod entered the chamber and advanced in a determined manner to the spot before the platform facing Hyrcanus. A wordless sound of admiration swept the room. For there the handsome Herod stood clothed in rich royal purple, rich jewelry glittering from his shoulder-clasp, heavy golden chain about his neck, his armlets, and the hilt of his sword. His feet were enclosed in gold-leathered sandals. His head was held high, perfectly barbered.

It was now the turn of Hyrcanus and the high priest to gasp, and that would be the last sound heard from them until after Herod had left the room. Where was the supplicating accused murderer, prostrating himself on the floor before them, begging for their mercy? This spectacle of the richly-clad defiant Herod was much too astonishing. But there he stood—glaring arrogantly into the face of Hyrcanus.

The bearded face of the high priest went chalky. Herod glared on. The mouth of Hyrcanus began to slacken and gape. Herod just stood there, feet wide apart, his right hand on the hilt of his sword. He boldly glared straight into the face of Hyrcanus.

The two hundred and fifty soldiers were ranged closely behind

Herod, cutting off any assault that might arise from the spectators; but now that threat had completely disappeared.

The lids of Hyrcanus's eyes began to flutter. His eye-balls
rolled higher and higher into the back of his head until his pupils
all but disappeared. His body shook with tremors. Herod stood
before him, daring him silently to open his mouth.

Now Herod, beginning at the extreme left of the circle of the
seventy high priests, looked into the face of each priest individ-
ually, and dared each one in turn to speak. Eyes were averted.
Heads dropped as if to examine something which had fallen in
their laps.

When Herod's challenging gaze reached the center of the line
again, Hyrcanus was not in his place. He had fainted from terror,
and slid to the floor. He lay there twitching his arms and legs in a
most fitful way. Not one of his colleagues dared to rise, and go to
his assistance.

Herod completed his examination of the entire circle. Not one
priest dared utter a word, let alone deliver an accusing speech.
The silence in the chamber was total.

Finally the spell was broken. Then several more let go their
breath. Now Herod stalked back to the place before the seat of
Hyrcanus, and spoke in an imperious voice.

"My generous nature permits you to escape my wrath this
time, but if you ever again interrupt my duties as governor of
Galilee again, you shall all feel the weight of my sword."

Herod then stalked from the chamber, his guards following
after, two abreast, in precise military rhythm and manner. They
emerged back upon the street to the wild cheering of thousands.

No account of what had happened in the chamber had yet
reached the streets. Herod's smiling appearance said enough.
The cheering could be heard all throughout Jerusalem.

Design by Eileen Callahan O Malley
and David Orion Callahan in
Mergenthaler Cloister with Cloister titling.
Printed by Maple-Vail.